HANDS ACROSS
TIME
The Soulmate Enigma

OTHER BOOKS BY JUDY HALL

Findhorn Press:
The Art of Psychic Protection
The Zodiac Pack

Other Publishers:
The Karmic Journey
Menopause Matters
The Astrology of a Prophet?
Principles of Past Life Therapy

HANDS ACROSS

TIME

The Soulmate Enigma

JUDY HALL

FINDHORN
Press

First published 1997
Reprinted 1997

ISBN 1 899171 61 4

British Library Cataloguing-in-Publication Data.
A catalogue record for this book is available from the
British Library.

Cover design and book layout by David Gregson.
Printed and bound by Interprint Ltd., Malta.

Published by
Findhorn Press
The Park, Findhorn, Forres IV36 0TZ, Scotland
tel +44 (0)1309 690582 • fax 690036
email thierry@findhorn.org
http://www.gaia.org/findhornpress/

For Rob
who has all the qualities of a true soulmate

Acknowledgements

I would like to thank everyone who gave me permission to use their stories. Obviously I cannot name you as that would break your anonimity, but you know who you are. My very special thanks go to Justin Carson and David Lawson, and much love besides.

I am grateful to Sue Boase for writing the stories of Diana, Joanna, Julia and Belinda. Also the publishers who so kindly gave permission to use extracts from published works (see Notes).

To everyone at Findhorn Press my love and thanks, especially to David for the cover design and Lynn for her sensitive editing as always.

Contents

To a Soulmate

When you came to my heart
I welcomed you in,
An innocent maiden
Unknowing of sin

And the three sisters spun
At the edge of the World
While our love came unbidden
Our future unfurled

Time circled about us
As shadows grew deep
While the web became darker
And tangled with sleep

Then you begged for my soul
For you'd none of your own
And I gave it you gladly:
Blood, flesh and bone

And the three sisters spun
In the black of the night
Whispering shadows
Cursing the light

Though I dreamed of redemption
In sunlight and rain
I had bitten your apple
And slept in my pain

At last your betrayal
Cut clean, like a knife,
Yet the husk of my spirit
Clung fiercely to life

At the edge of the World
The three sisters spin
And the price of my freedom
Is a knowledge of sin

—*Jane Lyle*

Soulmates
and how to avoid them

What love is, if thou wouldst be taught
Thy heart must teach alone
—*Friedrich Halm*

RE YOU STILL SEARCHING for perfect love, your 'other half'? Have you found your soulmate and are living happily ever after? Have you found your soulmate and wish with all your heart you had never met? Have you been surprised to meet several soulmates? You are not alone. The answer may well lie in another life, in another time. This book may help to explain why we so desperately seek a soulmate, and why so few people find it the blissful experience they expect. It will show you why it might perhaps be better to avoid your soulmate altogether, and how to take back your heart if you have left it in the keeping of a false soulmate. It may also help you to have a realistic enough picture of what a soulmate really is to attract a true companion of the heart.

Many people have wondered what attracted, and held, John Lennon in an unconventional and symbiotic relationship with Yoko Ono. Astrologer Pauline Stone (who was married to Lennon's father) put forward the psychological view when she surmised:

Perhaps John sensed that Yoko was the perfect embodiment of his anima, and that through her he would become complete in a way that had never been possible in his former relationships with women.[1]

John himself expressed it differently:

Before Yoko and I met we were half a person. You know there's an old myth about a person being one half and the other half being somewhere else, in the sky or somewhere, like a mirror image. But we were two halves and now we are whole.[2]

He believed that he and Yoko were the reincarnation of Napoleon and Josephine and other famous lovers. In his eyes they were two halves of the same soul, bonded throughout eternity:

Two souls with but a single thought
Two hearts that beat as one

—*Friedrich Halm*

Soulmates

Ask most people what they mean by a soulmate and they will reply 'the person who makes me feel complete', or 'my other half'. They are convinced that there is only one soulmate for them, and that when that soulmate comes into their life, it will bring them everything they have ever wished for. They will live happily ever after. For those who believe in reincarnation, this soulmate will be someone with whom they have shared life after life, almost certainly as lovers. Indeed, people often describe feeling their soulmate reach out to them across the centuries. Poets are particularly good at catching this evocation of past love:

You have been mine before -
How long ago I may not know;
But just when at that swallow's soar
Your neck turned so,
Some veil did fall, – I knew it all of yore

—*Dante Gabriel Rossetti*

Other people feel it too. In *Bridge Across Forever* author Richard Bach asked: 'Did you ever feel that you were missing someone you had never met?'[3] and went on to relate how he sought out his deeply yearned-for soulmate for many years before they met and, finally, married.

Psychiatrist and past-life therapist Dr Brian Weiss wrote a book *Only Love is Real* detailing how two of his patients searched the past for their soulmates only to find them in each other:

In separate regression experiences, both were reconnecting to exactly the same lifetimes, but lived from a different perspective. Although they came from very different backgrounds, and had never met, they seemed to share a common history. Across many lifetimes, they appeared to have loved and lost each other time after time.[4]

When, finally, they passed each other in his waiting room, there was a backward glance, but that was all. No instant recognition here. On this occasion, destiny was at work. The two met and fell in love on a plane high above America. They married and now have a child. As the Indian poet Tagore says:

> *We two shall build, a bridge for ever*
> *Between two beings, each to the other unknown,*
> *This eager wonder is at the heart of things.*[5]

Countless people have caught a glimpse of someone and known they were fated to meet, their eyes met across a room and that was it... As Shakespeare says in *As You Like It*:

> *Your brother and my sister no sooner met, but they looked; no sooner looked, but they loved; no sooner loved but they sighed; no sooner sighed, but they asked one another the reason; no sooner knew the reason, but they sought the remedy: and in these degrees have they made a pair of stairs to marriage, which they will climb incontinent, or else be incontinent before marriage.*

Others have searched diligently for their own true love. Many have found what Brian Weiss describes as 'profound bliss and happiness, safe in the knowledge that you are together always, to the end of time.'[6]

But..!

Whilst this scenario may well happen and you may find exactly the right person to make you feel profoundly loved and fulfilled, over twenty years of exploring karmic relationships leads me to believe it is not always this simple. Yes, I have had couples in my consulting room who, separately and together, have relived life after life where they were together. All the details clicked. The interaction was clear. But these were usually couples who had consulted me because of difficulties in their relationship. Soulmates can drift apart over the period that is eternity. Even when they meet, they may not necessarily reunite. One may recognise the other, but be spurned. Karma is a cycle of action and reaction. What goes round, comes round. Karma is dynamic; we may need to experience a myriad facets of love. We all have lessons that our soulmate willingly enters into with us, experiences that we share.

Finding a soulmate can bring us new life, but it can also ultimately bring death. The writer Arthur Koestler and his third wife Cynthia had been happily married for almost twenty years when Arthur began deteriorating rapidly. He was suffering from chronic depression, leukaemia and Parkinson's disease. He and his wife believed in voluntary euthanasia to prevent further suffering. In a *Guide to Self Deliverance*, a Euthanasia Society pamphlet, Koestler had written: 'Euthanasia is a means of reconciling individuals with their destiny'. Now he felt it was time to leave life.

Cynthia, although much younger than Arthur, did not want to be parted from him in death. At the inquest she was described as being devoted to him, living in and through him as wife and companion, secretary and housekeeper. Her whole life was bound up with him. She could not live without him. So they died sitting quietly together over a bottle of pills and some whiskey.

On the other hand, the almost middle-aged poet Elizabeth Barrett, a reclusive opium addict who had been slowly dying from a chest complaint for twenty-five years, found new life when courted by the somewhat younger Robert Browning. She had hardly left her room in all that time. Elizabeth's tyrannical father had not allowed any of his children to marry and would not allow 'courting' under his roof. Any lover affairs his adult children conceived had to be kept strictly under wraps. The Barrett–Browning courtship was conducted, initially, by letter.

Elizabeth at that time was a well known and much respected poet, Robert an up and coming one. She mentioned Browning in one of her poems (Lady Geraldine's Courtship). His picture was already on the wall by her bed, so we can surmise an attraction to him was already at work. Indeed, one of her friends was later to insist that Elizabeth was in love with him long before they met. Certainly when Robert wrote to her, ostensibly about her poem, he declared his love for her. This was not love at first sight:

it was love before meeting. In that first letter he says: 'I do... love these verses with all my heart and I love you too'. Even making allowances for the flowery Victorian style of prose, it is a pretty direct statement. Elizabeth replied the next day: 'I thank you, dear Mr Browning, from the bottom of my heart'. They clearly had a powerful connection. Over the next twenty months they wrote each other 574 letters.

When they finally met, five months after their correspondence began, Elizabeth found her 'ideal man fleshed out'. The visit unsettled her. She could not sleep, despite her opium. She could not get him out of her mind – alien feelings, for a woman who had led such an emotionally sheltered life (although she was no stranger to emotional trauma; it was her beloved brother's drowning that led to her prolonged illness in the first place). Robert, on the other hand, was much more straightforward. He was in love and declared so again in the letter he wrote immediately after that first visit. In a later letter he was to say: 'My heart will remember'. Hearts played a great part in their relationship, as with all soulmates. The poetic lines which had put them in touch in the first place have an allusion to the heart:

> *Or from Browning some 'Pomegranate' which, if cut deep down the middle, shows a heart within blood-tinctured of a veined humanity.*
>
> *(Lady Geraldine's Courtship)*

Years after Elizabeth's death, Browning told a woman who pursued him: 'My heart lies buried in Florence' (Elizabeth's last resting place).

Within months of their meeting, Elizabeth had moved from a virtually bedridden invalid to someone who could suddenly go out and about; marry secretly; travel with her new husband to Italy, where they would spend the next seventeen years; and even give birth to a son. It was the first love relationship either had had. Robert never remarried after her death. He remained a widower for twenty eight years. As Elizabeth said: 'If God choose, I shall but love thee better after death'.

A collection of poems *Sonnets from the Portuguese* came out of this union. These contain what is perhaps Elizabeth's best known line: 'How do I love thee, let me count the ways'. But they also included a poem which, in its first draft, was entitled 'Death or

Love'. This was the choice Elizabeth had had to make – to continue under her tyrannical father's rule and inevitably wither and die, or to take up her unlived life, marry her soulmate and experience love. She chose 'Not Death, but Love'.

What they both found was a mature love that expected and demanded nothing from the other. As she said: 'If thou must love me, let it be for naught Except for love's sake only'. Like so many soulmates before and since, they knew each other intimately from the start. From the letters it is clear they shared thoughts and feelings without words, although words did, of course, instigate their love. But it was what lay behind the thoughts that mattered most to them. They shared 'intuitions of the heart'. There were no barriers between them. As Elizabeth put it: '[I] am inside of him and hear him breathe'. Robert said: '[we] know each other for time and, I trust, for eternity… we know each other.' And yet, at the same time they remained individuals and of independent thought. They did not lose themselves in each other totally, but they accepted each other absolutely. An old friend told them: 'If two persons were to be chosen from the ends of the earth for perfect union and fitness, there could not be a greater congruity than between you two.'

However, even in this most blissful of marriages, dark clouds blew. There were disagreements, most noticeably over Elizabeth's espousal of Spiritualism, of which Robert disapproved. Elizabeth was prone to deep dark depressions, as well as her physical illness, and these, although much lessened after her marriage, continued to plague her. She was deeply affected by the loss of key figures in her family and sought solace in contact with them.

This brought another woman into the picture – not for Robert but for Elizabeth. She came under the spell of Sophie Eckley, her 'sister in the spiritual world', a soul sister who idealised and idolised her. The two shared a mutual interest – the spirit world – but the friendship went far beyond this. Their letters declare their love – a love which, on Sophie's side, was obsessive and, as it turned out, deceptive. Her false soulmate revealed, Elizabeth had to break free. She wrote to Sophie breaking off the contact. Her marriage was renewed. But is it perhaps an echo of Sophie we hear in Browning's lines:

If two lives join, there is oft a scar.
They are one and one, with a shadowy third;
One near one is too far.

The eternal triangle often arises in soulmate relationships, as we shall see. After Elizabeth's death, Robert wrote in her bible these lines from Dantes's *La Vita Nuova*:

Certain am I – from this life I shall pass into a better, there
Where that lady lives of whom enamoured was my soul.

Dante was, of course, another poet inspired by a soulmate. The divine Beatrice, glimpsed, adored, but never possessed. He met her when he was nine, and then again at eighteen, but her memory stayed with him for the rest of his life. His idealised love for her was the inspiration for his work. After her death, Dante married but his wife did not accompany him into exile, so it can be inferred that the marriage was not an ideal relationship.

Our present lifetime may not always be the point at which we are destined to be together again. This may be the point at which we have to break off the relationship to go on to new things. We may be seeing the 'negative face of love'. But still we yearn for our soulmate. As John Masefield, a former Poet Laureate, foresaw:

I know that in my lives to be
My sorry heart will ache and burn,
And worship unavailingly
The woman that I used to spurn
And shake to see another have
The love I spurned, the love she gave.

Our soulmate may be a 'psychic vampire' who has been feeding on our energy for centuries and will continue to do so, if we allow it. A gothic horror tale may not be the first thing that comes to mind when thinking about soulmates, but in the 1992 film *Bram Stoker's Dracula*, Dracula loved his wife more than life itself. They were soulmates. On being told false rumours of his demise she threw herself into the castle moat. Given the news, Dracula vowed to overcome death – to live until he could be with her again. He became, by sheer force of will, a vampire who fed off the blood of livings beings, taking their lives to sustain his own. It was his way of taking revenge on God and on humanity for allowing such a thing to happen, and of sustaining his soul until he could be reunited with her.

When she is reincarnated again, Dracula moves to England to be near her. He tries to lure her into his world. Fascinated with her old love, whom she recognises at a soul level, but torn between him and her new love, only Dracula's death can save her. To live, she has to be party to his release from this world. But it is a painful choice. It is no wonder the Dracula story has proved so popular down the years. It embodies a psychic truth: the undead can prey on the living. An old soulmate contact can suck the life out of someone. But equally, an old desire for revenge can keep someone, or something, alive. One day we too may have to let go of the past for the sake of our soul.

When I give talks on soulmates, I always ask how many people are searching for their soulmate. A forest of hands goes up. I then ask who has found their soulmate. Many hands rise. In response to the question: 'And how many of you can honestly say you are truly blissfully happy?' most of them go down again. Quite a lot go back up when I ask: 'And how many of you wish you had never met your soulmate?' After we have had a few examples of why, most of the first group of soulmate seekers have changed their minds!

Hundreds of my clients have asked: 'I found my soulmate but I've been put through hell. Why?' So often clients say to me: 'I've found my soulmate but he, or she (it happens to men as well), does not want to know me'. As we shall see, a soulmate contact from one life may not necessarily carry over to the present life. It may not be on the soul's blueprint this time round. As we shall also see, you may not meet your soulmate for the purpose you imagine.

So often the soulmate we knew in one life, has changed, put on a different personality. He or she, we complain, is not the same person. Of course not. We all have to develop and grow, and change is a fundamental part of this process. This is the purpose of reincarnation. We incarnate again to change ingrained patterns, to experience the opposite of what we have been, to make reparation for what has gone before, or to learn new ways of being, to develop another side of ourselves. So, someone who was our soulmate in another life, may not be appropriate any longer. They may have come back into our life now for a different purpose. If we immediately act on the 'wave of lust' that so often accompanies a soulmate recognition, we may find ourselves in bed with someone with whom we intended to work in some way, with whom we had a 'mission'. Having been to bed with them may not hinder this, but on the other hand, it could do – especially if one or more soulmate already has a partner. As we all belong to soul groups, we may find ourselves in a new and different relationship with a previous soulmate: they may be our child, our parent, our grandparent even. The relationship cannot then be the same as it once was.

The search for a soulmate, or the memory of a previous life association, can so often wreck ordinary relationships. The search for perfection is a lonely, loveless road. People who spend their whole life searching for their soulmate, and rejecting other relationships in the process, should perhaps bear in mind that Plato, in his explanation of twin souls, says that one being split in two and ever the twain shall wander seeking each other. He does not say they will necessarily be united again, only that something will impell them across lifetimes to search for each other.

Origins

In Plato's *Symposium*, which sets out this picture of soulmate origins, Aristophanes says that human beings were originally two persons in one body, with two heads and four arms and legs. In their completeness and satisfaction, they rolled along in ecstasy, ready and able to do almost anything. They had overweening pride and formidable strength and vigour. This led them to attack the gods. Not wanting to kill them outright, Zeus (the then Head God) split them in half, thus diminishing both their powers and their happiness, and forcing them to spend their lives yearning for the missing half.

> *Each half yearned for the half from which it had been severed. When they met they threw their arms around one another and embraced, in their longing to grow together again, and they perished of hunger and general neglect of their concerns, because*

they would not do anything apart. When one member of a pair died and the other was left, the latter sought and embraced another partner, which might be the half either of a female whole (which is now called a woman) or a male.[7]

Plato points out that:

It is from this distant epoch, then, that we may date the innate love which human beings feel for one another, the love which restores us to our ancient state by attempting to weld two beings into one and to heal the wounds which humanity suffered.[8]

This is the origin of soulmates.

Plato may well have based his concept of soulmates on an ancient Egyptian tale. When Ra created the first god-beings, Shu and Tefnut (as the Larousse Encyclopedia of Mythology euphemistically says: 'without recourse to woman'), they were a divine pair. Their children were Geb, the earth god, and Nut, goddess of the sky. Originally these two were closely united, rather like siamese twins, both brother and sister and husband and wife. But Shu, on the orders of Ra, split them violently apart and held Nut high in the sky. Ever afterwards, Geb was inconsolable and his lamentations were heard day and night. His body became the earth, her body the sky. He is usually pictured with a huge penis reaching up towards her. His longing for her is acute. Ra, who had them separated when they married without his consent, forbade them to have children. But Thoth, the tricky god of wisdom, gave them five days of the moon's light, days that did not belong to the official calendar. During these days Nut was able to bear her five children and Geb's longing was assuaged. During the remaining 360 days of the year, they were parted.

Sexes

Plato says there were originally three sexes: male, female and bi-sexual hermaphrodites. Each male was split into two males halves, each female into two female halves, and each hermaphrodite into a male half and a female half. The male halves then sought their twin soul in another man, the females in another woman, and the parts from the hermaphrodite in heterosexual union. So, in this view, a soulmate does not necessarily have to be of a different gender. We have just as much chance of finding our soulmate in homosexual relationships as in heterosexual ones.

Manifestations

We can see in Plato's description of what happened when two parts of the one soul found each other again one of the major pitfalls of the soulmate experience. The two became so enamoured of, and reliant on, each other they would perish from hunger. In a way, this is what happened to Arthur Koestler and his wife. She could not go on without him. This kind of 'total union' can, contrary to popular belief, sometimes be totally disempowering and, as we shall see, it may be necessary for one half to get out of the relationship in order to survive.

Years ago, I met a woman at a party. She knew nothing about me, but spent the whole time telling me about her problems in relationships. A couple of days later she knocked on my door. 'I don't know what you do,' she said, 'But whatever it is, I know I need it, right now.' When I explained that I sometimes took people back into other lives in order to find out the meaning of what was happening in the present life, she said, 'That's it! Do it!' She didn't want to tell me why in case it influenced what I did, so we went straight ahead with the regression. One of the inductions I use is to open a door and step through into the other life. As soon as she stepped through, she gave a great sigh of contentment:

Mmmm… I'm in the most beautiful garden. It is so peaceful and tranquil here. I can hear the bees humming in the flowers and there are birds singing. I am sitting on a seat under an apple tree, just looking at the garden. In the distance I can see a small house. This is my home. It is so beautiful. Quite perfect. I am so happy with my life.

Now I am waiting for my husband to come home. We have only been married a year. Here he comes [great excitment in her voice]. *He is so dear to me. We are so happy. I love him so much. He is here, he is kissing me. We sit in the garden and take tea. Life is so perfect.*

Being a bit of a cynic and thinking this regression was all too perfect – an illusion maybe? – I asked her to move forward in time:

As the years pass we grow more and more in love. We are so happy, so content with each other. We do not have children, but we don't need them. We have each other.

Eventually I took her forward to her death:

I am in bed. I know I will die soon. He sits and holds my hand. He wants me to be with him forever, but I know it is my time to go. He kisses me and I fall asleep. I never wake.

I asked her if she needed to do anything else: 'No,' she said, 'I know what I came to find out'.

When I brought her out of the regression her comment was:

Do you know something, it was all so perfect, so wonderful, and so very very boring. I didn't learn anything, I didn't grow. I didn't do anything with my life. I thought at the time love was enough. But it wasn't. And now I'll tell you why I wanted to do that regression. I have met a man. He seems to be perfect. We get on so well. He wants to marry me and spend the rest of our lives together. We seem to be soulmates. But somehow I don't want to. I couldn't think why. It was what I had been looking for all my life. But now I know. He is the man from that other life. I would be bored and I couldn't stand that again. I want a relationship that helps me to grow.

In my experience, a past-life regression may not be to an actual, factually true, lifetime. But it is a symbolic and psychic truth – it is the way our soul communicates to us what our psyche has experienced and is still experiencing at some level. This woman had experienced 'true love' but it was not enough. Deep down inside, she knew that the soulmate experience she so longed for could only take place through her own inner integration, not from someone outside herself.

But, in time she forgot that. Her need for companionship became so strong that she married a man who looked after her to the extent that he hung up her clothes for her as she took them off, and even took the top off her boiled egg before she ate it. He had retired and they did everything together. At first they were blissfully happy, soulmates – she said. After a few months of marriage she was going up the wall. 'I just can't stand it. I feel stifled, I have no life of my own. I have to get out. This is not what my life should be about.' She needed to get back onto her soul's path.

There is considerable experiential evidence to show that we do not have just one soulmate. We all have several soulmates with whom we have been in many different relationships in the past. Regression to other lives shows that we take on many roles within loosely knit soul groups, any member of whom may feel like a soulmate (or, our greatest enemy) when we meet up again. The relationship may also change roles, or the beloved return again in some new disguise:

> *Speaking through the babe now held in her embrace*
> *She hears again the well-known voice adored:*
> *'Tis I, – but do not tell!'*   —*Victor Hugo*

Soulmates are not an either/or situation. They can be wonderful and they can be terrible, and they may be both at one and the same time. They may also start as a blissful experience and end in trauma and pain. Occasionally, the reverse happens. Sometimes the pair come through a traumatic beginning and find peace together. One half of the 'pair' may recognise the other first and will do all in their power to help the other come to a realisation. Quite often, the one has to support the other through some highly destructive experiences – and in the process learn that you cannot do it for another person. We may find a false soulmate, or one we are attempting to extricate ourselves from. So often though, we are caught in a repeating pattern of interaction, stuck on the karmic wheel. We go into the relationship because we have always been in the relationship, and on and on. This situation feels comfortable because it is so known and familiar. There comes a time, however, when we must change the pattern, step out of the known. At other times the roles alternate, the persecutor becomes the victim, the victim the persecutor, life after life. Repayment and reparation are an endless round. Again, we must step out, break the cycle of the past.

...and how to avoid them?

Why should anyone want to avoid their soulmate? After all, isn't this the very person who is going to make your life complete? – to bring you the happiness you have been seeking all your life? Maybe, maybe not. Whilst positive soulmate contacts are to be desired, so often we meet a 'false soulmate' who brings havoc into our lives. This may be a part of our soul's purpose. It may also simply be that we are caught up in a repeating pattern. Stepping out of that pattern gives us the opportunity of reassessing our part in it. Are we blindly following our past, or is this where we can move ahead and grow?

If you easily fall instantly in lust, but believe it is true love; if you find yourself thinking 'Oh no, here we go again', or cannot understand why your soulmate wants nothing to do with you, then it may be better to learn how to avoid soulmate relationships for the time being. By stepping out of the pattern, taking a deep breath and asking 'Is this really love or is it just pressing my buttons?' instead of tumbling headlong into yet another disaster, you may gain insights into why you have attracted this person. You can identify the patterns behind your emotional need for 'another half'. In time, you can find that other half inside your own self. Taking a whole person into a relationship then totally changes the outcome. Once need no longer drives the search, there is every possibility of finding true love.

The whole soulmate experience is much broader than popular belief would have us think. My clients and I have explored so many facets of the soulmate experience over the past twenty-five years that I felt it was time to share in more depth the enigma of the soulmate connection. In doing this, I will use case histories which are true but in which names and minor details have been changed to protect the confidentiality of my clients. These case histories have been selected because the experiences they embody have been repeated over and over again by clients in regression or in their everyday lives. In essence, these are all our stories. They are part of the journey of our soul. In the last analysis, relationships are where we meet our self in another. They are the mirror of our being:

Your encounter with partnership tells you who you are,
not whom you should avoid.

—*Tom Bridges*[9]

My clients come from all walks of life: medicine, law, the army and the arts, agriculture, science and ecology, social work, teaching and commerce. There's a pop singer or two, actresses and actors, university professors, consultant psychiatrists, psychotherapists, journalists, writers, people on social security, members of the aristocracy, diplomats and even a member of parliament. You will find their stories together with those of historical figures, and most probably your own story, here. The soulmate experience is universal and ubiquitous.

Your Soulmate

friend or foe?

*Fear and hatred are the most powerful magnets in drawing souls
together to complete unfinished business*
—*Pauline Stone*[10]

What is a soulmate?

Twin souls, twin flames, soul partners, soul companions, soulmates.
There are many words to describe these beings who make us feel
so right, as though we have been waiting for them all our life – or
lives. So, what exactly is a soulmate? Well, a quick look through
three best selling books on the subject produced three remarkably
similar pictures:

In *Soulmates,* Thomas Moore sees a soulmate as someone to whom
we are 'profoundly connected', something which is brought about
by 'divine grace' rather than an intentional act on our part.[11]

In *The Bridge Across Forever*, Leslie Bach (wife of author Richard
Bach) describes a soulmate as someone who has a lock to which
we have the key, and we in turn have a key to fit their lock. With
this person we can be our true self. They bring out the best in us.
We share with them a purpose, direction and 'our deepest
longings'.[12]

Speaking of soulmates in *Only Love is Real*, Brian Weiss says a
soulmate is someone who crosses time to be with us, someone
whom we instinctively recognise from our heart. Someone to
whom we are 'bonded throughout eternity'.[13]

When Gordon Craig met his soulmate, the exotic dancer Isadora
Duncan, he said of her in 1904:

> *Our meeting first of all was... a marvellous coming together...
> Suppose one had been in a world with one's other half – once – and
> that world so wonderfully perfect, and then suppose that world had*

dissolved and time had passed over one, and one had woken up in another world – but one's other half not there. One would have taken to the new existence as cheerfully as possible… Then, suddenly, the marvellous happens – that other half is standing beside one; she has found her way, after all these centuries and over all those hills and rivers and seas – and here she is – and here am I. Is that not marvellous?.. with what a cry we come together.[14]

Isadora said of that meeting with Craig in Berlin that she had been psychically aware of him all evening (he was sitting in the front row of the audience). When the performance was over, 'there came… a beautiful being.' But, he was angry; accusing her of stealing his ideas and scenery, he said she was the 'living realisation of all my dreams'. Isadora responded that they were in fact her designs, which she had invented when she was five years old. But Craig insisted they were his and that she was the living embodiment of the dream being he had created them for. The mystery, apparently, was solved when she found out that he was the son of Ellen Terry, one of Isadora's great childhood heroes – her ideal of womanhood. Craig wanted to spirit Isadora away from her family, so that she could be with him. 'Like one hypnotised', she allowed him to put on her cape and take her away. When they eventually reached his studio, she said:

All inflamed with sudden love, I flew into his arms with all the magnetic willingness of a temperament which… waited to spring forth… In him I had met the flesh of my flesh, the blood of my blood… Hardly were my eyes ravished by his beauty than I was drawn toward him, entwined, melted. As flame meets flame, we burned in one bright fire. Here, at last, was my mate; my love, my self – for we were not two, but one, that one amazing being of whom Plato tells in the Phaedrus [sic], two halves of the same soul… This was the meeting of twin souls.[15]

This is the most usual view of soulmates: one soul, and one soul only, who makes us feel complete 'for ever'. A couple who are bonded for eternity; an ideal – or should it be idealised – relationship. Within a few weeks of meeting Gordon Craig, Isadora Duncan found it was her 'fate to endeavour to reconcile the continuing of my own career with his love' – an impossible combination. When she found she was pregnant, she was ecstatic.

Craig was unhappy: 'My work, my work,' he would despair. The baby brought her great joy, him deep gloom. Isadora knew, despite the great love she had for him, that they would separate. Some twin souls find it impossible to live together.

From my perspective, a better definition of a soulmate would be: '*A soul companion who helps us to grow*'.

The growth may entail some extremely hard lessons indeed, as we shall see, and our soulmate may just be the person with whom we go to hell and back – not as a punishment but as a learning process. As one of my clients said: 'Our soulmate is the person who is here to teach us the hardest lesson'.

I prefer to look on it as helping us to learn, rather than being taught, a difficult lesson. And, I would add that our soulmate is the person who loves us enough to put us through some painful situations – and to be with us through some difficult times. Several soulmates have found their 'other half' just in time to see them through, or be accompanied to the end of, a terminal illness. It is clear from regressions to the 'planning stage' before incarnation that such lessons are frequently, but not always, knowingly sought. It is also clear that members of our soul group agree to participate with us (we all have many such soulmates). But we may forget all this when we come into incarnation. It is, however, also apparent that other people can become caught up in our soul dramas unknowingly, and play their part accordingly. They may appear to be a soulmate, but the recognition is spurious and premature. Finding a false soulmate can be a bit like feeding the endorphin receptors in your brain with chocolate, valium, etc. For a time the 'fit' is good and the body is fooled, but gradually it becomes obvious that the substance/false soulmate is addictive and deadening rather than life-giving and consciousness-enhancing.

Our own inner expectations play their part too. We attract what we expect, and it feels comfortable even though it hurts like hell. As fear, hatred, rage and old resentments are powerful magnets in mutual attraction, they draw us together again to complete the unfinished stories of our former lives. No one soulmate is enough to fulfil all these needs. Nor is a soulmate relationship necessarily 'for ever'. It is for as long as it takes.

Where did it all begin?

The answer to this question can only be symbolically described at best. At worst it can lead to deeper confusion. In my experience, words only limit our understanding. They do not add to it. We have already looked at Plato's view (see Figure 1). We can also look at other esoteric ideas about the soul in its many facets.

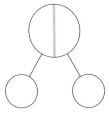 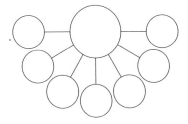

Figure 1. Twin Souls   Figure 2. The Oversoul and its Satellite Souls

In certain schools of Hinduism, there is the concept of an 'oversoul', which has several facets in incarnation at once (see Figure 2). These facets are rather like puppets controlled by the oversoul, so that they gather the experience it is seeking. When two of these facets meet, they are attracted to each other and feel like twin souls. When the facets move out of incarnation, they take back to the oversoul all they have learnt.

In the Western Mystery Tradition, a pool of spiritual essence contains the whole. A piece of this 'breaks off' – the soul group – and then continues to subdivide into individual souls. However, the parts can come together again to unite and reunite, sharing all that has been learned (see Figure 3). This is the interweaving web of soul connections. Each part of this web will feel like a soulmate, some more strongly than others depending on how far from the original branching the souls have moved and on the experiences they have had together in former lives. So, souls A and B will probably recognise each other, and may feel like soulmates. G and H will be 'soul companions', one in incarnation and the other guiding from another dimension. E and F will probably feel like soulmates if they meet. But will C and D? They have come a long way from the original split. From experiences in other lives, they may feel like powerful enemies. Love and hate

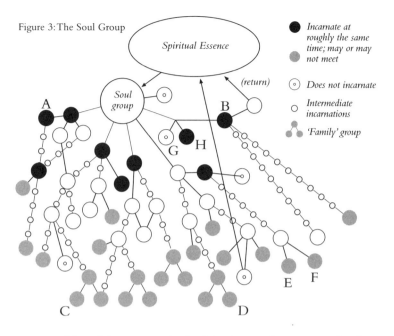

Figure 3: The Soul Group

Spiritual Essence

Soul group

(return)

A
B
G
H
C
D
E
F

● Incarnate at roughly the same time; may or may not meet

◉ Does not incarnate

○ Intermediate incarnations

'Family' group

are two sides of the same coin. In this picture, there are souls who will never incarnate on earth at all. They act as 'guides' or soul companions. This is the picture I personally find most helpful.

Whilst not everyone we meet will be part of our soul group, it is likely that all important contacts, whether they be fleeting or lifelong, will be with someone from 'our group'. In this view, our parents or wider family, friends or partners, may or may not be from the soul group. It all depends on the impact they have on us. It is possible to choose a family for the genetic and emotional inheritance rather than a soul connection – although we usually find at least one member of our true soul group within the family to support us in our early years. It is possible to be attracted to a partner because he or she embodies patterns and traits with which we are all too familiar. They feel comfortable, and safe, even when they are far from being so. It is also obvious from regression work, that we can belong to more than one group. Some people act as a link between groups – and maybe if we trace the connections back far enough, we will find that the two apparently disparate groups are in fact one.

How to recognise a soulmate?

I looked up and into the room walked Linda. Our eyes met and something just went wham in both of us... She is the most caring, loving, supportive human being... She was, is, and will always be, the most wonderful friend and partner anyone could ask for.

—David Icke[16]

- Did your eyes meet across a crowded room?
- Did your heart pound?
- Did you feel a sense of instant recognition? Of overwhelming love?
- Did you feel great, inexplicable antipathy?
- Did you want to run, somewhere, anywhere?
- Did it feel like a large magnet was inexorably pulling you onwards?
- Did you feel a wave of lust? Or revulsion?
- Is someone in your thoughts all the time?
- Were you especially close to one of your parents?
- When someone went away did you feel like a part of you had left too?
- Do you feel like someone is punishing you?
- Do you have a compulsion to be with this person, no matter what?
- Do you feel you will die if you have to part?

If you answer yes to more than two or three of these questions, the chances are you have found a soulmate. Typical scenarios include:

'I caught a glimpse of this man, just one look. I have spent the rest of my life trying to find him again. I know we are meant to be together.'

'I saw the back of his head, just for a moment as he walked along the street. I knew this was the man I would marry. Eventually we met. We married almost immediately. The relationship has not been easy however.'

♥

'I was on holiday. I saw him sitting at a table at a cafe. I knew I would speak to him. Then I panicked. What if I was mistaken. Just to make sure, I went for a long walk to give him time to leave. When I came back, he came straight up to me. We talked for hours and have never been apart since.'

♥

'All my life I had been looking for someone, my 'ideal woman'. When I met my wife, I knew I had found her. But now she wants a divorce. Why?'

♥

'I went out with her when I was in my teens. Somehow, I could never forget her. Then one day I met her in the street. I grabbed her hand. That was it, I just could not let go. We began a passionate affair. I left my wife, but she would not leave her husband. I still cannot let her go. We meet when we can. I love her so much. Why does my soulmate treat me like this?'

♥

'The first time I saw him my heart pounded, I felt sick and my legs shook. I was terrified of this man, and yet I had never seen him before in my life. I found myself married to him. I was never quite sure how it happened. It was like I was hypnotised.'

♥

'No matter how hard I tried, no man could ever match up to my father. My mother was very jealous of our relationship. I felt she hated me. In a regression, I discovered I had once been married to the man who was now my father. I had had him first, no wonder she was so jealous.'

So often the 'love at first sight' scenario includes 'feeling like I have known him, or her, forever'. We may pause, take a step back, try to rationalise or escape. But inevitably we find ourself in a relationship. And equally often, it is followed by difficulties in the relationship as we get to grips with the lessons we have come together to learn, or we replay out our old patterns.

Equally we may find ourselves compulsively attracted to someone we know is 'bad' for us. When we first met we may have felt inexplicable fear or rage. But somehow we find ourselves together in relationship. Our soulmates are not only those people who love us the most. We may have to learn forgiveness and compassion through interaction with an old soulmate who has reason to hate us, or whom we have reason to fear.

Illustration: The First Meeting

We may also find ourself going through these same lessons or patterns with someone who is not our lover. It may be a friend, an employer, a family member. Yet, when we met, it felt so right. How is it that we can replay the same power struggles, parental patterns, emotional games and so on in so many contexts? The answer may well lie in the past, in our previous contacts, or in the expectations we bring to our present life.

It is the intensity of the experience, coupled with the fact that the memory never fades, that is the key to recognising a true soulmate experience.

The psychological scenario

Psychology has an answer to the riddle of soulmates. In the psychological view, there is an inner being – the anima or animus depending on whether you are male or female. This inner being is the opposite gender to the body you inhabit. It contains all the 'ideals' we have internalised (and quite a few less desirable qualities too) of the opposite sex. When we meet someone who embodies exactly these qualities, we recognise them. We say: 'Here is my other half'. In other words, our soulmate is a projection of our deepest desires, fantasies and expectations – our dream lover incarnate in flesh.

So long as the projection continues, and the other person does not intrude themselves into the picture, we will be satisfied. But as soon as they become an individual to us, someone other, disillusionment sets in. They are no longer perfect, simply because they are no longer reflecting our ideal back to us. With a nice twist, they then reflect back to us the undesirable, or unacknowledged qualities in ourselves that we have been trying to hide from all this time. Whilst our soulmate may offer us an irresistible opportunity to know our self, we may nevertheless resist with all our might. We feel that they have let us down rather than recognising that what we sought was both a fantasy and our inner self.

Astrologically speaking

There is an astrological explanation for soulmates. An astrological chart is a picture of ourselves. It is a moment frozen in time: our birth. It describes our inner dynamics, our expectations and our past. It has many dimensions. Some astrologers look to past lives – karmic astrology; others only take the current life, but all will say that the chart shows how we approach love, what we want from relationships, and how we expect love to be. These are indicated by the placement of the planets and by how they interact with each other. Very often, the chart will show that we have conflicting feelings about love. One part of us expects one thing, another part something quite different. We are all complex characters.

Although our own particular birthchart is unique (only someone born at exactly the same time and place has the same chart), charts can exhibit certain similarites. Planets can have the same internal relationship to each other, they can interact in the same way, or live in the same 'house'. We do not need to go into technicalities here. If we do have a chart that is similar to another person's, depending on how many connections there are, we may feel as if we know that person from the inside.

I once worked for my astrological twin (someone born on the same day but at a slightly different time and place) for some months without actually meeting him. He would leave cryptic notes, ring me from call boxes, and somehow the work got done. I instinctively knew what he needed. No one else could understand how we managed it. When we met, it was on our mutual birthday. When we compared notes, we had had similiar lives and shared many interests in common. We had the same attitude to things. We looked at life through the same glasses, as it were. Not surprising really from an astrological perspective, so much of our chart was exactly the same. Any differences between us were accounted for by the different times of our birth and the resulting slight difference in our charts. We were close friends for many years and felt like soulmates. I have never met anyone else who understood me in quite the same way. He could tell me what made me tick, and I, him.

There are also more general characteristics we can share with other people. Someone with the same Sun sign will approach life in the same way. We will share the same natures. Aries, for instance, are fiery people who approach life head-on. They explode easily in a temper, but quickly forget it again. Two Aries coming together may be like two rams locking horns, but equally they can share a passionate interest in life – and in each other. If we share a Moon placement, we will feel in a similar way and have the same emotional response to life. We may also share certain inherited characteristics or attitudes because the Moon also corresponds to the past and what we inherit from our ancestors. If we share a Venus placement, then what we are seeking from relationships will go along similar lines. Our approach to love will be the same. So, if we meet someone with these shared characteristics, they will feel familiar. The more connections there are, the more complex relationships within our own chart we share with someone else, the more we will feel 'I know this person'.

When we combine our chart with that of a lover, it describes how the relationship will function and what each will bring to the relationship. In soulmate relationships, certain astrological connections invariably occur. Our personal planets, especially the Sun, Moon and Venus, tend to contact planets like Neptune in the other person's chart. Neptune has few boundaries. It is the urge to merge with another person. We can share the same thoughts and feelings, even when we are not together. We feel like we are in that person's skin with them. This is the dream lover personified. Under a Neptune contact, we can be spellbound, hypnotised, illusioned, disillusioned.

Whenever someone says to me 'I know this is my soulmate', there will be at least one, and probably many more, contacts with Neptune. As a karmic astrologer, to me such contacts reveal that these people have been in close relationship to each other many times in the past. No wonder they feel so close now. But, of course, there may be other things in the chart that reveal that, this time round, they have not planned to stay together. They may be working on different issues and have another purpose. There may be Uranus contacts across the charts. Uranus is electric, magnetic – and chaotic. It is the planet of freedom and change. It is also the planet of sexual ecstasy, but how much one soul can take will depend on the factors in the natal chart. Whenever we have strong Uranian contacts with someone, one of the issues that arises will always be 'Do I commit to this relationship, or seek my excitment elsewhere?' Uranus does like to keep the options open. Pluto is different again. The planet of power, Pluto likes to be symbiotic and obsessive. Pluto contacts are much more difficult to sever, but we may suffocate under the weight of them if we are not careful.

It can be painful when we meet such a soulmate and have to move on. On the other hand, there can be different aspects which indicate that yes, no matter how problematic the relationship feels, these people are destined to be together. Saturn, the lord of karma, likes certainty and boundaries. With Saturn you know where you stand: 'We have to work through this; it feels like we made a promise to do so' is the most common response to Saturn contacts. This planet is the glue that holds relationships together – or the ball and chain that imprisons us, depending on how you look at it. We will look further at how astrology can illuminate relationships later in the book.

Sex and the chakras

The chakras are energy centres along the spine, rising from the base chakra at the bottom up to the crown chakra at the top of the head. These energy centres form the link between our physical bodies and the more subtle levels of our being. They lie along the pathway that the kundalini takes as we open up our spiritual – and our sexual – energies. Kundalini is our 'inner fire', both raw sexual energy and a spiritual force that resides, until awoken, in our base chakra. Eastern yogis have always stressed the importance of right preparation before kundalini is awoken, as otherwise the consequences can be dire.

The chakras play an important part in soulmate relationships. The base and second chakra are closely connected to our sexual organs and can be opened through sexual intercourse. With the right partner, all the chakras will open and the kundalini flow during sexual congress, leading to a true union on the physical, emotional, mental and spiritual levels of our being – the mystic marriage. With a past-life sexual partner, or with a false soulmate, the bottom chakras only will light up but the kundalini can still ignite. One treatise on Tantra says that the kundalini is likely to be stimulated and awakened by sexual contact as the life energies merge. This is an unmistakable experience. There is a rising tide of 'liquid fire' that is both hot and cold, lightening and liberating. It is an electric feeling that almost paralyses as it takes the breath away and opens up the whole being.[17]

Despite all that the church, and others, have taught over the last 2000 years, such sexual energy has its place in spiritual work and may well be why soulmates seek each other so assiduously. Whilst celibacy may be one way of attaining a spiritual peak experience, sexual experience is equally valid. Millennia ago, sexual energy was recognised, and utilised, for spiritual growth. The kundalini force, when approached with proper reverence for its power, could take one to the spiritual heights – instantly. Tantra is one of the remnants of this age old teaching. However, in the hands of the inexperienced, the kundalini force could blow someone apart, physically, emotionally, mentally and spiritually. So, the unfolding of this power was in the hands of those who were trained to understand it. Knowledge was withheld from the inexperienced, not to gain control, but to prevent harm. Sexual magick was a part of the esoteric teachings revived at the beginning of this century by metaphysical organisations such as The Order of the Golden Dawn. (We will look at the experiences of two initiates later.) For the most part, although there are genuine masters trying to revive this knowledge, these highly trained beings are no longer available, especially in the West – but many false gurus have tried to take their place. So, humankind is now left to find its own way. But the old forces are still there.

Powerful, and often inappropriate, sexual attraction is one of the pitfalls of the spiritual and soulmate path. Men and women who are developing their intuitive and spiritual faculties find themselves compulsively attracted to, or attracting, sexual encounters of a destructive kind – especially when control over this force has not been mastered. Some people have a magnetic sexual charge, a sexual frisson that touches everyone around them (look at some of the great actors or actresses and some of the more enduring 'pop' stars).

A past soulmate will have this same effect on an old partner. So often, the first meeting with a soulmate is accompanied by a wave of lust as our lower chakras burst open under an irresistible force. The challenge is to transform the energy, to bring it to a different way of functioning, to be truly creative on the level of the spirit, coming into union with the self. We may not be meant to jump into bed to immediately discharge this energy, nor should we just ignore it. So often the energy is repressed, only to rise again even more strongly.

One only has to read the early desert-dwelling church fathers to see how obsessively they dreamed of sexual temptation, and, today, some priests and guru-figures hold a particular aura of sexual magnetism for certain women – and men. Sexual charisma holds an aura of power, and power is open to abuse. Contact between priests and choirboys regularly makes the front page of the tabloids, as do bishops and their love affairs. Gurus and their disciples make the news less often, but the attraction, or the abuse, can be the same. It can be an irresistible, inextricable mix of the sacred with the profane, the forbidden with the greatest temptation. One does not have to be a priest or guru to carry this air of 'forbidden fruit'.

Over and over again, when people describe their first meeting with their soulmate, the common thread is overwhelming sexual desire. When I began my work with Christine Hartley many years ago, she explained this kind of soulmate attraction as the result of the opening of the chakras and the rise of the kundalini energy. It literally results in a magnetic attraction to the powerful emanations of the kundalini force, and, because the soul is involved, it feels like the highest spiritual experience. In some cases this is so, and the sexual interaction is appropriate.

When I met my present partner twelve years ago, we stood under an old olive tree on an ancient temple site in Rhodos. It was the night of the full moon. Without even touching each other, we both simultaneously experienced a rush of the kundalini force up the spine and out the top of our heads: a kind of 'cosmic orgasm'. We have an explosive Uranian contact across our astrological charts and this was one of its more positive manifestations. The energy was channelled and harmonised in each of us, creating the mutual fire. Several psychics have described our being together in that particular place thousands of years ago, when it was a working temple. It certainly worked its old magic on us that night.

In other cases, the attraction is inappropriate. Unfortunately, people find themselves pulled into this kind of sexual attraction and try to justify it by saying that it is spiritual – the instructions being received 'from a higher plane' when in fact it is the repressed and denied side of their own sexuality. Like so many things, it is difficult to judge from the earth perspective exactly when such an interaction is appropriate and when it is not. In my case, my partner and I knew that we had to be together, that we had work to do, as well as old karma to work out. One result of that initial union was a 'cosmic child', a book we wrote together. We often work with the same people, approaching their difficulties from opposite directions but both, ultimately, working to help their soul find its proper expression. Ours was not an easy passage, but we made it. However, in cases where people come together purely for self-gratification, or to exert power over another person, it would seem that future karma must accrue and the passage will be even rougher.

In the book *Initiation*[18], which Christine Hartley gave to me many years ago, Elisabeth Haich connects the potential for spiritual union, at a soul level, with the desire for sexual intercourse and says that it is the unsatisfied longing of the soul for 'paradisical union' that lies at the heart of the dissatisfaction and fatigue that many people feel after sexual intercourse. She also points out that the higher someone rises in their spiritual evolution, the higher their vibrations become, and the more irresistible their emanations become to other people. (Such an attraction may be misused by false gurus, as we shall see.) She highlights the need to control the flow of spiritual energies through the body as otherwise the nerve centres (what I would call the chakras) can be damaged by the flow of untransformed energies into the lower centres. In the book, the High Priest tries to warn the initiate of the result of such an unrestrained act. But, with deep feeling with which I am sure many people would be in total accord, the initiate points out that: 'The best advice cannot change inexperience into experience, and my inner lack of balance and self-control had to be brought back into equilibrium through painful experience.'

Karmic lessons

In many ways, we bring our relationship disasters or joys upon ourselves. This may be a positive, constructive choice because we have recognised that we need to learn certain lessons or change certain ingrained patterns of behaviour – although it rarely feels positive whilst we are going through the lesson! So often, we can only appreciate what we learnt in these kind of situations with the value of hindsight, and that may have to wait until we move on from the present body. On the other hand, we may be so caught up in that old ingrained pattern that we unconsciously re-create it time and time again. Abuse, misuse of power, abandonment, rejection, domination-submission, and many other such scenarios have a powerful hold over us simply because they are known and familiar. In other words, they are compulsive. They are rarely conscious and we may agonise over where we went wrong, how we came to be caught up in such scenes.

But go back to another life, then another, and another... and the chain of events becomes plain. It is only by compressing and intensifying this experience, bringing it to a point past bearing that we break out of the pattern – or away from the person – and find a way to move on.

A variation on this theme also comes up rather frequently: one life one way, the next life the opposite way. In other words, swinging between two poles of the same experience. Somewhere, somehow we have to stop and find the point of balance.

We also find that we are getting back what we put out. If we abused, we become abused; if we were abused, we become the abuser. If we manipulated, we become manipulated; if we were passive, we become dominant. If we abandoned, we are rejected, and so on. It is rarely black and white. The person we treated so badly may either come back to us in the role of abuser, or we may find that we have to care for them. They could be our child, for instance. We may also find ourselves having to care for a child who, in another life, murdered us, abused us, made our life hell. We could also find ourselves married to that person. The confusion comes in when, despite all this, this person could still feel like our soulmate. Indeed we may have been attracted for this very reason. Our lesson is to change the pattern of interaction, to forgive, to let go, to love unconditionally.

After my partner and I had been together for a few years, a psychic who happened to be visiting us did a karmic reading on our past. He picked up a life in ancient Egypt. I had been a young, rather obnoxious princely being. My partner had been my slave whom I treated very badly and he had hated and despised me as a result. Rather than walk, I insisted on being pulled around the palace in a little cart – by my slave. In an uprising, my slave took the opportunity to stab me in the chest and kill me. Neither of us have any memory of this, nor any animosity. What is interesting is that my partner is a rather different sort of doctor. One of the things he has been helping me to heal is a longstanding chest problem, my karmic wound as I have always called it, exactly at the spot where the psychic saw the knife going in. What is also interesting is that, when in Egypt, a place where we both feel most at home, we spend a great deal of our time travelling in a calèche – a horse cart – together.

One of the most frequent causes of relationship difficulties is old vows and promises carried over from the past. Our soulmate may be here to help us break free of these vows and move on. Religious vows are an obvious difficulty. So many people have had past-life experiences in a monastery or convent. They vowed poverty, chastity, obedience – for ever. Then they wonder why they are always poor, have sexual difficulties, and are constantly waiting for someone to tell them what to do, or are powerless, at the mercy of someone else's will. When a soulmate comes along, they willingly surrender their life and then find that the lesson is to take control for themselves.

We do not necessarily have to go into another life for this, but the present-life experience is usually itself an echo of a former life. I have seen several experiences where people have been drawn back into a convent or monastery in the present life, or lived as though they were in one.

In one case, a woman felt she simply had to be a nun. She went into the convent and took her vows. For her, Christ was her beloved soulmate. It took her twenty years to realise that she had made the wrong choice. As soon as she came out of the convent, she caught sight of the man who was to become her husband – her soulmate. It took several years before they married, despite the fact that she 'knew it had to be'. Even then, she came under considerable sexual confusion until she deliberately rescinded her vow of chastity. Up until then, she felt subtly 'wrong' and wanted to run back into the sanctity of her beloved convent. She knew she had taken a vow, but just imagine how much stronger is the effect of such a vow lived out for a whole lifetime, or even several lifetimes, and then forgotten at a conscious level. Deep down, the soul does not forget. The person holds back, cannot give of their self in a relationship because, at the innermost level, it is 'wrong'. Where a soul partner understands this and is patient, it may be possible to overcome that vow. but so often the experience hooks into the other partner's greatest fear – rejection, lack of love, etc. – and an old pattern is reactivated. Unless the two people then consciously work at healing the past, even the closest of soulmate relationships finds itself in trouble.

In a similar story, a young monk came to see me. He had converted to Catholicism at the age of fourteen. He then went into the novitiate at a famous monastic boys' boarding school. One of his reasons for going into the monastery was to leave his sexuality behind – he was strongly pulled to homosexual relationships but felt them to be morally wrong (he hadn't read Plato). On his first night in the monastery, he was brutally raped by one of his fellow monks. To enter into full 'monkhood', he did not have to take a vow of celibacy, simply to make a protestation of faith in order to be accepted. It was understood that celibacy was part of his new way of life. However, the rape was the beginning of a seven-year sexual relationship, one full of abusive rage and domination. But, as he said, he had found his soulmate. He was torn between expressing his sexuality through this sado-masochistic contact or denying his soulmate.

In the end, the monastic leaders took action. He was sent back out into the community 'to find himself'. However, when returned to the everyday world, he was totally lost. He felt like a part of himself had stayed at the monastery with his soulmate. He also found it impossible to enter into any new relationship, he was still bound by the ideal of celibacy that he had been unable to keep within the monastery. The result was a very lonely life indeed.

There are other kinds of vows: 'One day he'll know how it feels', 'I'll get my revenge on you', 'I'll never forgive you' are powerful links that draw souls back together. In these cases the marriage vow of 'For better or worse' usually turns out to be the latter. The promises we make also draw us back: 'I'll always look after you', 'I'll love you for ever', 'Whenever you need something, just come to me' can hold us in thrall throughout lifetimes. We need to revise the past – to set ourselves, and the other person, free.

One of our major lessons can be that of letting go. Whether it be a person or a pattern, the past cannot be repeated endlessly. Stagnation and inertia are death to our soul. So, we find ourselves in the situation where we meet a beloved from the past, only to lose that person again. In this respect, death can be a great teacher.

Or we meet a soulmate who is already happily married, or who is a child, a teacher, a brute. Whatever the interaction, we are inextricably bound up within it. Until we let go, we experience hell on earth. When we finally let go, we blossom.

Letting go of our illusions is another challenge. We may need to re-vision, to see the other person (or belief) in a different light. If we have been used to putting a partner on a pedestal, idealising and idolising, then we have to recognise that any other human being we encounter is also mortal, not a god. We have to let other people reveal their true nature, not assume that we know it. If we give them an heroic, idealised role, there is no way it can be fulfilled. We will inevitably find our illusions shattered. Just as when we entertain illusions about ourselves, eventually they must fall away so that we see ourselves clearly. This applies equally to where we see what other people, or ourselves, can be, rather than what is now. If we invest in, or project onto, other people what we are not yet ready to own in ourselves, one day we will have to take it back. Such a taking back can be done in a positive fashion, or it can be through the painful breaking of the shell of our illusion – a brutal psychic rape that hurls us into the essence of what we are. In the depths of our despair, we can either clutch at someone else, or find our own strength.

All lessons can be learnt in a positive, constructive fashion, or we can fall back into a destructive pattern. A great deal depends on how much conscious planning we have done in advance. Say our soul lesson is to find greater independence. The positive experience would be through soul partners or parent-child, teacher-pupil type interactions which are supportive and encouraging of self-responsibility and self-reliance. Gentle urging into new ways of being has no criticism, no judgements. We are allowed to develop at our own pace, knowing that we have loving support behind us. We can make our mistakes, and learn from them, without incurring wrath. We may be challenged when it is appropriate, but this will always be done with compassion. When we are ready to fly on our own, we are encouraged to go. We go out into the world confident and well prepared. This applies just as much to a partner as it does to a child. If partners are unafraid, confident in themselves, then they can encourage their partners to be their own person. If they are afraid, they will clutch on, trying to keep them as they were and restraining growth.

The destructive, negative approach to achieving independence is 'heavy', narrow-minded, critical and cold. Disapproval, fear and punishment are used to force a break – although a break is the last thing the cold, critical person wants. They want to maintain control over this downtrodden soul. We have to leave for our own survival. We have to listen to the urging of our soul. We may achieve self-sufficiency, but it is at the cost of lifelong (or lives long) resentment of authority figures, usually accompanied by a deep feeling of inferiority and lack of confidence. If this lesson is being learnt within a marriage, it is doubtful indeed that it will survive this approach. If it is within a parent-child relationship, then the child may well leave home and never return.

The Varieties
of karmic relationship

The heart has its own reasons which reason knows nothing of
—Pascal[19]

Relationships are a fruitful, exciting and sometimes painful way of learning and growing. Our present-life experience is seldom enough to fully explain our relationships. We can look to other lives for the roots of our relationship patterns. For convenience sake I call these past or previous lives, but these should not be looked at as strung out in a long line behind us. Our 'past' lives are all around us. We meet them everyday. It is these hidden influences that draw us to a soulmate.

We need to look at relationships in the widest possible sense of the word: interaction with another, as even the most fleeting contact may bring us a karmic lesson or present an opportunity to grow. Soulmate contacts tend to be catalytic. We may meet one of our soulmates just once, for a short time only, but the interaction will mark our soul for ever. Sometimes a soulmate comes into our life for just one purpose – to do whatever it takes to propel us into what we may be. Sometimes they point us to a lesson we need to learn. Such lessons may not be earth-shattering, but they can change our life, as Ann found when she met Jim:

About fifteen years ago I was in the USA visiting friends, Carol and Adam. Shortly before I was due to return home they invited an old friend of theirs over for dinner. I had heard a lot about this man, Jim, from my friends, and perhaps this could have had something to do with the instant 'knowing' I felt when I met him. I still have a photograph of that evening, and all I can say is that there is a glow about that picture. However, I was due to leave the following day, so that seemed to be that.

The following morning I called the airport to confirm the time of my flight, and was told the flight had been cancelled and there was no other flight for two days. The shock and confusion I still felt from the night before resulted in my smoking several cigarettes (I am a confirmed non-smoker!). As a 'New Age' person, I asked myself what this could mean, and decided that it meant I was to spend more time with my new friend from the night before. I told Carol I would phone him, and was told that he was impossible to reach by phone. I was determined to try and dialled the number – and Jim answered! A negligent secretary had left the line directly through to his office! Carol was astounded, but by this time the coincidences were becoming commonplace.

Jim invited me over that evening and we talked well into the night. It was a most extraordinary time. I felt so open. I liked him so much. I have no idea if he felt the same. I do know that we could talk openly and vulnerably about any subject. I was afraid that he might think I was making a pass at him (he was married). The strange thing is that of all the deep subjects we discussed the only one that sticks in my mind and has helped me to change my life view was very mundane. He told me that he was a very tidy person, the rest of his family were not, and there were constant conflicts and arguments between them. One day he made the decision that the problem was his; he was the one who wanted a clean and tidy house, so he decided solving it was also his. Since then he had tidied up after the others without blaming. He felt better because he had what he wanted; everyone else felt better; and the household became harmonious and peaceful.

So what have I learned from this simple lesson? That when I have a problem, I also have the solution. It's as simple as that.

On return home I was tempted to write to Jim, but had a strong feeling that this was not the right way to go. I released the whole experience, and felt completely comfortable with that. Yet whenever I feel myself blaming others for my problems and difficulties it comes back in a flash.

I don't know if Jim is my soulmate, although this has been my belief for the past fifteen years. I do know that he made an important contribution in my life. I don't want to glamorise the meeting, but, added to various other inner 'knowings' that I have experienced this lifetime, I trust this feeling. There have been and are, other relationships in my life far more intense and with stronger long-term impact. Still I *feel that there was something about Jim, about our short meeting, that was somehow familar and known.*

There are other people in my life I feel strong links with, I don't know what I believe about soulmates, but I am open to the possibility that I am part of a group, or that there are some people incarnated now that I have spent other lifetimes with. And yet, somewhere inside me I still feel there is something special about Jim.

Strangely enough, Jim came back into my life recently. I spoke to him on the phone and may meet him again sometime. Part of me does not want this to happen, I wonder why?

At another time, our soulmate comes to work on the karma that exists between us. Karma is all that has gone before. It is action and reaction, credits and deficits. It is also potential, where we can grow. Whilst there is positive and 'good' relationship karma, it is the destructive, negative patterns that create most of the problems people encounter in their relationships, especially on a soulmate level. Part of our reason for being here is to recognise and reverse these patterns. Once a pattern becomes consciously acknowledged, it can be changed by choosing to respond differently rather than blindly reacting in the same old way. We can become proactive instead of reactive. It is our soulmate (or mates) who are most likely to help us in this endeavour.

Earth is the place where we work on our emotions. It is the only level of existence where we can 'hide' our emotions. Communications from other levels, especially that 'closest' to the earth, describe emotions as instantly visible by colour, emanation, etc. So, the earth is where we may fool ourselves, and try to fool others, about our emotional state. It is also the place where we can gain emotional equilibrium. Relationships, or lack of them, are of course the vehicle for much of our emotional experience.

Karmic relationships fall into two distinct types:

1. Relationships based on a prior soul contact where themes or experiences are carried over and continued in the present life; and where our 'worst enemy' may well turn out to be someone with whom we have a strong and loving soul link. This is the soulmate contact. Here the karma is personal to the two people concerned. These relationships fall within our

'soul group' – a group with whom we have had long connections and within which all relationship interactions have been experienced. Soul links can bring people together to undertake a specific task, to deal with unfinished business or to repay debts and obligations, to act as a catalyst, or to spend a lifetime together.

2. Relationships in which we have no prior contact with the person concerned but where we are both working on a particular theme or pattern, and so we come together to try to resolve it or fulfil the potential of the contact. This is where we might feel we have met a soulmate because the contact feels so right, but it is more likely to be a false soulmate contact. It is plugging into all our old comfortable 'relationship receptors' and the other person is mirroring our most intimate self back to us through their innate patterns. But, the connection is rarely there at a soul level. We may sometimes create it through our relationship, but it is not an inherent factor in that relationship.

Karmic themes

In our relationships we tend to act out certain themes over and over again. Typical karmic themes include:

Father/mother/child – roles which are rarely anything to do with the actual family relationship and which carry over from the past into other interactions. We all know the woman who is her husband's 'little girl' – or his mother; the father who flirts with his daughter whilst relegating his wife to 'mother'; the mother who cannot let her son go; the child who has to parent a parent. We see marriages where the two people concerned are more like brother and sister, somehow the sexual element is missing or weak. The personal assistant who mothers her boss and the employer who expects to be mothered are familiar themes – and can be played out by men as well as women. We are perhaps less familiar with the secretary who calls on her boss to act a parental role, although it does happen. As these roles are so known and familiar and so often form part of our previous soul group connection, it is easy to slip into them inappropriately. They often form part of the spurious soulmate experience.

 Victim/martyr/persecutor/rescuer – frequently the rescuer ends up as the victim or martyr. Abuse and misuse of power, sometimes in an extremely covert way, is fundamental to this type of karmic interaction. In a family, one child may be made the family scapegoat, picked on by everyone. The rescuer/victim role is common in families where addiction of any kind is a problem and one or both parents or siblings take on the 'helper' role, but it happens in so-called love relationships too. As one need matches the other, it can so easily feel like a soulmate contact. Co-dependent relationships of all kinds are based on this pattern. They cannot function without one person feeling inferior to the other. But need is strong on both sides. A victim needs a persecutor, a rescuer needs someone who cannot help themselves. If someone is continually helped, 'rescued' or persecuted for being 'weak' they can never find their strength and the pattern endlessly repeats – often down through generations.

 Dominance and submission – a power and control issue. It may literally re-create an old 'master–slave' type of interaction or be a metaphor for power trips of all kinds. It is based on the need of one partner to be dominated, and the other to dominate. If the scenario is played out unconsciously, then there may well be considerable violence within the relationship, especially where the person with the need to be dominated unwitting evokes the domination, or where the formerly submissive partner begins to assert his or her own power. Common in parent-child interaction, the parties may be drawn back together to re-enact an old dance which has become a set piece. This is why so many abused partners find it difficult to leave situations of domestic violence: like it or not, they crave the security of the known and familiar domination. It is important to recognise that it is not only the dominant who abuse, the 'meek and mild' too may be tyrants in their own way and skilled at pressing the buttons that erupt into violence. Of course, it is well recognised that the children of abusive relationships often go on to abuse as the wheel turns and they experience the opposite polarity.

The healing in such relationships comes when the dynamics are recognised and each makes a conscious effort to incorporate the other end of the polarity rather than simply reacting blindly. Role play or role reversal may be needed to fully understand what is going on – this may be experienced through another life. Learning mutual trust is also an essential ingredient as is hearing the other person's needs and finding a creative outlet for the mutual power play.

 Dependence and collusion v. unconditional love – two ends of the same axis. So often collusion and dependence masquerade as 'helping' or being helped. People believe they are practising unconditional love when they give someone whatever they appear to need or want. It may, however, be better for their spiritual growth to stand back and let them find the way, or to say no and mean it. Such 'helping' tends to disempower rather than enable someone to take hold of their own power.

Unconditional love means accepting someone totally, warts and all, honouring their unique way of growing, letting them be what they need to be. Equally unconditional love means knowing when to say 'No' – and stick to it! It does not mean allowing someone else to walk all over us in the name of 'love' or growth. It does not mean allowing them to abuse or misuse us – or abusing or misusing them in the name of 'love' – patterns which can entwine down through a family, or a soul group. Loving someone unconditionally may also mean challenging the way they are, their assumptions, their actions. They may need to be brought up short, to face consequences. But with love. This is the hard and rocky path of the soulmate.

 The betrayer and the betrayed – so many promises made, so few kept. This theme is obvious in adult relationships where one of the parties takes a lover, often repeatedly. It is less obvious in family situations where a child is encouraged along a pathway only to have support abruptly withdrawn. So, for example, an only child may be the apple of his mother's eye, but when a new child is born, all interest is lost in the first. He, bewildered and alone, finding that he is no longer the centre of the universe, then carries into his adult relationships both a lack of trust and the desire to dump someone before they have a chance to dump him. If a child is continually promised something, only to be disappointed, it will set up the betrayer pattern in adulthood. If the pattern is carried over from other lives, the parties involved may interweave a tapestry of betrayal over many lifetimes. Nevertheless, one soul can feel deeply bound to another by promises made and lost.

 The enabler and the enabled – so common in addictions of all kinds, this interaction is also found in many so-called soulmate relationships. It feels like a soulmate relationship because 's/he needs me so' and 'I can't do without him (or her)'. It is common in marriage partnerships where the wife puts all her energy into her husband's career rather than her own, or in parent-child relationships where the child follows a path of dependency, fueled by the parent's money. One person inevitably puts in all the energy, or creates exactly the situation in which the other person can flourish or wither according to orientation – usually in a 'weakness' or dependence of some kind, thus keeping the enabler in power. Such a pattern has a tight hold over the parties, who believe they cannot survive separately. It can also be a covert relationship, the seeming enabler is just as likely to be the enabled when the relationship is subjected to the bright light of understanding.

The seducer and the seduced – often based on a past love relationship, the soulmate connection can be abused and misused in friendship, love and family. Seduction is not always sexual. It is often intellectual or emotional and can be spiritual too. This pattern is also common in guru-pupil interaction. The guru (spiritual or otherwise) seduces the pupil by seeming to know, and keeps the control by parcelling out just enough of the knowledge the seduced is so desperately seeking. Of course, in so many guru-pupil relationships (and other types too), the emphasis then switches to a sexual sharing, often in the name of passing on power but in reality to binding the seduced ever closer. This again is a theme that travels across centuries.

- **The freedom-commitment dilemma** – the 'can't live with him, can't live without him' theme played out over many lifetimes. Some relationships are sporadic, exciting, highly passionate – so intense that they could not possibly be sustained for a whole lifetime. If left together for too long, the partners become bored with each other, the relationship burns out, or one partner may run out on the other, unable to take on full responsibility in the relationship. The two partners concerned may choose to have a life together where they learn how to commit fully. To do this, they need to give each other space: space to grow, to be, to do whatever they need but within the framework of a committed relationship. The urge is to flee, to fly into freedom, but the soul says 'No, wait'. Or, they may come together to learn to live apart, to finally let each other go. If partners have always been heavily committed to each other, symbiotically entwined, dutifully bound, then the lesson may be to let go, to find freedom – to learn to love another, or another way.

- **Positive service** of some kind – a strong feature of soulmate relationships. The parties have agreed before incarnation that one of them will perform a particular service. This may entail looking after someone who needs an illness or disability in order to learn compassion and empathy, but it may also be the so-called handicapped person who is performing the service. Rudolph Steiner says people with handicap have taken it on not as a learning experience for themselves but as a gift to others, so that they might learn. If someone has a particularly hard task ahead in the outside world, then a soulmate might take on the role of support, offering a loving relationship within the home; or a parent might prepare a child as well as possible for adulthood.

- **Reparation** – reparation may be made or received. Guilt can be a powerful force in repeating karmic interaction, but reparation can also be made in a positive fashion. It entails repaying past debts or honouring agreements made in other lives. So, for example, if someone has offered us an opportunity to learn and grow in a past life, we may put our own development on hold for awhile to support them. Equally, if we have harmed them in some way whilst learning our lessons, then we may want to make things better for them in the present life. This can lie behind parent-child or mentor-pupil relationships. It is also found in marriage and other love relationships too.

The family

Our earliest relationship is with the family:

> *We life and breathe in the energy field that our parents create through their relationship with each other.*
> —*Stephen Arroyo*[20]

We choose our family for the genetic and emotional inheritance they offer us. We may have prior contact or old karma with individual members of the family. One or more of our old soulmates may well now be our parent or sibling. The whole family may be part of our soul group but this is not necessarily so. Remember, your true family is a soul group who are linked not by blood but by 'respect and joy in being in each other's life'.[21] It is not necessarily the case that members of such a soul family live under the same roof.

The family relationship reiterates and reinforces our deepest expectations and beliefs, positive and negative, carried over from previous lives. We may well be continuing an old pattern we have become locked into. For instance, if we expect bad parenting, this is what we will notice, even if we have perfectly adequate parenting ninety percent of the time. On the other hand, if we have had and now expect good parenting, we can more easily cope with inadequate parenting (for a time). If we carry low self esteem, we will most likely attract parents who reinforce this by valuing us for what we achieve rather than for who we are intrinsically. If we have high self-worth, we are much less likely to be damaged by difficult early relationships.

If we have incarnated expecting to have (or needing to have) a particularly difficult childhood, we often find that a grandparent is a soulmate. We have that one person who seems to understand, even when everyone else does not. This can become a problem if the bonding is too tight. A woman consulted me because her granddaughter and she were so very close. The mother, her daughter, had split up with her partner just prior to the child's birth. Depressed and unable to cope, she handed her child over to her mother. Although the mother kept in close contact with the child, it was four years before she was ready to take her home. In this time, she had found a new partner. The child, given no time to adjust, hated her 'new father'. She was uncomfortable with her mother, did not feel safe, and desperately wanted to stay with her grandmother. In a rage, the mother, jealous of her mother's close relationship with her child, dragged the child away and then would not let them meet.

The grandmother was in despair. She really felt that a part of herself had been torn away. She was in telepathic contact with the child, and I suggested that she use this ability to 'talk' to the child to reassure her that she had not abandoned her – that she would be with her on other levels, especially during sleep (children naturally accept such ideas), but that, for the time being, they would not be able to meet. We also did some tie cutting (see Appendix I) so that the child would be set free from all the grandmother's expectations but would still be loved unconditionally. The grandmother used appropriate flower essences (see Appendix II), on a photograph of the child to help her adjust to the new situation (a useful technique when they cannot be given directly).

Eventually, she was able to talk to her daughter and reassure her that she did not want to take the child away, only to love and support her during this difficult transition. Gradually her daughter came round and in time allowed visits. With the new freedom, grandmother and granddaughter were able to spend their 'special time' together, and the child gradually began to enjoy family life with her mother and stepfather.

Family relationships can be complicated by previous life sexual relationships between the parties. Mother and son, father and daughter, or siblings, may have been husband and wife in the 'past'.

Recognising, and accepting, the old contact can go a long way towards explaining otherwise inexplicable interaction, inappropriate 'love', emotional or incestual abuse, etc. in the present life.

For instance, one of my clients was locked into a symbiotic, emotionally incestuous relationship with his mother. His father had died in his teens and his mother told him he had to take his father's place. This he had struggled to do for many years, and it spilled over into his adult relationships. His mother broke up every relationship he had. She simply would not let go. She treated his girl friends as though they were adulterous relationships, which, of course, from her perspective they were. He had taken his father's place, therefore they were taking her rightful place as his partner. He, on the other hand, was terrified of his mother. He could not stand up to her.

In desperation he undertook a regression. Not surprisingly, he went into a life where he was married to his mother. In that life he had a mistress whom he loved more than anything. He did his duty, as he saw it, and stayed with his family, but his wife knew that he did not love her. She made his life hell and eventually forced him to give up his love, taking punitive measures against her over which he was powerless to intervene. After that, his wife was possessive in the extreme, never letting him out of his sight. At social gatherings she made his life miserable with her jealousy and accusations. Time and time again she made him promise: 'You will love only me.' As far as she was concerned, he was her soulmate and belonged to her. She had carried this expectation forward into their mother-son relationship.

These childhood patterns are then carried forward into our adult relationships.

Adult relationships

Despite all our romantic notions, our efforts to find a soulmate, our adult relationships are often painful. It is hard to believe that we would willingly put ourselves through this but... as Mavis Klein says:

> Our intimate partners are deeply and knowingly chosen for the particular pains and joys that relating to them brings us.

We attract pain in an attempt to exorcise it. We seek out a painful situation because it is familiar but this time we hope it will end differently. Pain in our intimate relationship challenges the fixity of our personalities; and joy in our intimate relationships is the fulfilment of our ideal self.[22]

We attract in our partnerships soulmates, and others, who resonate to our patterns, who slot into our particular receptors. These receptors relate to our expectations around love. Expectations that have built up over many lifetimes and are deeply ingrained in our being. 'Love' themes that we may be dealing with include:

 The madonna/whore dichotomy. This is sacred versus profane love. (Too many nights spent in a monastery or convent can underlie this difficulty.) The fundamental problem here usually stems from a search for perfection (and incredibly high expectations of ourselves and others) and from seeing sexuality of any kind as 'bad'. The beloved is placed on a pedestal, idealised, idolised. When he/she behaves like a mere mortal fallible human being, total disillusionment sets in and the whole edifice comes crashing down. I so clearly remember one of my first clients telling me that marriage was for procreating children. Love was something different again: it did not involve sex. In her previous life she had been a nun who was sent into a convent for refusing to marry the man her parents had picked out for her. In her present life she had a husband, whom she did not love, and, having had a child with him, she refused him further sexual relations. She also had a 'beloved' whom she could neither marry nor 'make love' with. Sometimes, a person will settle on celibacy as a way of avoiding the issue of sex and sexuality altogether.

Unconditional love is the antidote to this pattern – as is seeing all love, sexual included, as healthy, natural and divine.

 The emotional black hole. That there will never be enough love is the greatest fear. There is usually a long history of manipulative, abusive relationships where anything that passes for love is accepted and held onto because of the great fear of loss or lack of love. A desperately needy and greedy desire for 'love' underlies this pattern. For many people, abuse and anger become internally confused with love. It may be the only attention they receive. So, 'if someone abuses me, they must love me' can be an underlying theme. And, of course, abusers of all kinds so often use 'love' as an excuse for their actions. People with this pattern find it very hard to go back in time to a life where they were loved fully and unconditionally. They have become used to settling for second best, but the hunger for love intensifies, it does not lessen.

Learning to find love deep inside instead of seeking it from someone other – connecting to the divine or cosmic love that is within us all – and being able to give love secure in the knowledge that this source will never run out reverses this pattern.

🌐 **'Love has to be perfect.'** This one often prevents relationships from beginning at all. In this search for perfection, there is such a high expectation, such impossible ideals to be met, that no one can meet these standards. A man in his forties told me the other day of his increasingly desperate need to find his soulmate. But, he said, she had to meet certain criteria in looks, dress, intelligence – and it all had to be immediately obvious. 'If it isn't right right there at the start, it's no good. I just can't get interested'. Not surprisingly, he never gets beyond the first date, never gives himself time to get to know someone intimately, never lets a relationship develop.

Within a relationship, the need for everything to be so special all the time creates an enormous strain on both parties. There is no room for the 'mistakes' that help us to learn, no room to be human even. Perfect love does not account for off days or PMT. I had a client who told me that he and his wife only made love about once every six months: 'But everything was perfect. We went out for dinner, came back and played beautiful music, sensuously massaged each other, and then made love perfectly.' He also told me that they had desperately wanted a child, so everything was timed to her ovulation. 'Somehow it didn't happen, and yet when she left me and went to live with someone else, she was pregnant immediately.' When I suggested that maybe more frequent but slightly less perfect lovemaking might have been the answer, he simply said: 'I couldn't do it. It had to be perfect to work.'

The way to heal this problem is to learn, little by little, to set more realistic expectations; to give oneself permission to experiment, even to make mistakes – and then to recognise that there are no such thing as mistakes, only learning experiences – to loosen up and allow for spontaneity and fun; to allow oneself and one's partner to be merely human; and to find that this in itself is a wonderful thing.

 'I don't deserve to be loved.' Someone suffering from this pattern will settle for anything resembling a relationship. They will accept 'punishment', or prostitute themselves for the housekeeping, for instance, because they do not feel they can be loved; they are not worth it. This pattern usually involves looking to other people for approval and validation. It can also be linked to a dose of the 'poor me's': 'it is not my fault'; 'I cant help it'; 'I have no control over my life'. These themes are very common in victim mentality. One of the difficulties is that, offered love, such people cannot allow themselves to accept it because they think, 'If someone loves me, then they must be as desperate, useless and unworthy as me' – and so they reject the possibility of a healing relationship. Unfortunately, as with so many patterns, it is a self-fulfilling prophecy.

Learning to love oneself first, to find inner self-worth, and then to accept love from other people is the lesson here. Here too, connecting to our spiritual core reverses the destructive process. Also recognising that we create, and attract, exactly the relationship we expect at our deepest level.

 'Love hurts'/'If it isn't hurting, it's not working'/etc. This is a treadmill... we create what we expect... our experience reinforces our expectations... and on and on we go – another self fulfilling prophecy!

If we expect love to hurt, then we either attract those with whom we have had painful relationships in the past, or we attract someone with the desire to hurt, and our expectations are reinforced once more. If we feel it must be hurting to be working, then again we attract someone who makes this so. Our soulmate may be only too happy to oblige, especially if we have been locked into this pattern for lifetimes together.

Breaking the pattern, recognising that you are both entitled to and capable of fulfilling relationships is the only way to change this. Forgiveness, of self and others, helps as does letting go of the past.

'I don't need love.' Separation and isolation are a choice many people make in order to avoid the pain of loving. They are seemingly independent and strong, but may be running away from old pain which, because it has been suppressed, has a powerful hold. Unfortunately, even when someone with this pattern has at last ventured into love, at the least sign of any perceived slight or hurt, they will immediately run, or struggle and fight. It is a patient partner indeed who can introduce someone with this pattern to intimacy. Reconnection to the spiritual core and releasing the old pain helps here, but a basic need is to take the risk of connection with humanity as well, especially through a one-to-one contact. Old vows and declarations, such as celibacy, may need to be rescinded before love can flourish.

The planning department

In my experience, one of the main causes of anguish and pain in relationships (and life in general) is shoddy planning or a deliberate decision which has been forgotten once in incarnation. Both are linked to the planning stage prior to incarnation, the 'in-between-life'.

The place to which we go after death depends so much on our expectations, and on the level of spiritual evolution we achieve, but eventually we are faced with the possibility or the need to come back to earth to work on issues that can only be completed here. Some people bounce back into incarnation – especially if they haven't travelled very far in terms of either understanding or the after-death levels of being. Others consider the matter very carefully indeed.

From regression, it is clear that some people spend a long time planning their next life and especially their relationships. They ask members of their soul group to take on certain roles – some of which can be painful or harsh in the extreme. One woman went back to this stage and found that she had asked one of her soulmates to teach her about pain and rejection, which she 'needed to learn so that I could have empathy for others'. He was an exceedingly good teacher. Having apparently fallen head over heals in love with her, he walked out the door with no explanation and she never saw him again.

Other people in a similar situation find that their lover leaves through death so that they might learn strength and self-reliance, or even to open the way for another relationship to flower. In the Lennon-Ono relationship, for instance, when John Lennon died it may have been time for Yoko to become an independent woman again instead of the symbiotic half of a seeming whole. However, when John died, Yoko went immediately into another relationship – one which continues to this day.[23] Ironically, when John and Yoko had separated some time previously, it was she who had sent him away: 'To learn what he needed to learn.' This resulted in his eighteen-month-long 'lost weekend' with her secretary May Pang (which several commentators have seen as Yoko maintaining control over him even at a distance). By the end of that time, John was writing and performing as a solo artist again. He had regained his creative strength. But, when his wife called him to heel, he meekly returned to his 'other half'. 'Mother [Yoko] has allowed me to come home,' he told May Pang. He returned to the symbiotic mother-child relationship that had become such a habit. Maybe in that time neither John nor Yoko had learned the lesson of living independently. After their reunion they became even more symbiotic and John stayed home for five years to look after their son, Sean, who was conceived after their reunion. When he was once again ready to venture into the world alone as a solo artist, he gave in to Yoko's demand that the album be a joint venture. Immediately after it was finished, he was shot dead. Who knows what they had planned when in the between-life state.

We certainly cannot know from the perspective of earth. Someone whose lover had been physically cruel and abusive found that she had asked him to do this, so that she could learn to assert herself and say 'No, enough is enough,' something she had not learned in her other lives. In the end, she was able to thank him for his part in her learning process.

Some people, for whatever reason, omit this planning stage or make it sketchy to say the least. They are simply pulled back into an old interaction, often by one of those vows that says: 'I must be with him' or 'I will always look after you.' They rarely take the time to discuss with their soul group what would be the best way to grow.

Even when people appear to be taking an active part in the planning session, it is not always so. When I was examining the David and Linda Icke with Mari Shawsun eternal triange, I was shown the pre-incarnation planning meeting when they were deciding what to do in this life.[24] Everyone was sitting around a huge boardroom table. There were advisers and other family members present. Each individual was taking a great interest. There was much discussion as to how the objective should be achieved. Then, when the relationship between David, Linda and their children came to be discussed, suddenly Mari was staring out of a window. She seemed to be paying little attention, the details were passing her by. Although she seemed to agree to what was being arranged, I had the distinct impression that either she genuinely did not hear, or that she was deliberately blocking it out in the hope that what she wanted to happen, her own relationship with David, would somehow be rearranged when everyone had forgotten what was agreed (that is, when they were in a physical body). When it came to be enacted on earth, her view was that David and Linda's relationship was supposed to end when she came on the scene; whereas David and Linda say that they believed they would remain together. The confusion caused endless pain and not inconsiderable acrimony.

That we get what we most desire is one of the karmic laws. This sounds great until we remember that decisions like 'I want to be with him/her next time', especially when taken at the moment of death, are a powerful desire that gets manifested, but without some between-life planning as to exactly *how* and *in what relationship*, the consequence is likely to be disastrous. Life can be acted out in a very literal way. My favourite story in this regard is the woman who vowed during a regression: 'He's going to marry me next time.' She burst out laughing and said, ' He did. He was the vicar.' She was lucky, most people find it's someone else's husband or wife, their child or that of a friend; or that their intended soulmate is of the same sex; or there is a huge age difference, and so *ad infinitum*.

We may have made a promise to look after someone, to be with them, without really considering the long-term consequences. We may need to redefine the karmic contracts we made. To renegotiate the concept of 'for ever'. One of my clients could not break free of looking after her alcoholic sister, who relied upon her for everything. For many years her sister took up all her time. Having eventually married and now in her early forties, my client felt that she wanted a child, but somehow her sister was her child and needed so much looking after she wondered if she would have the time and energy for a child of her own. They were caught in an enabler-enabled scenario from way back. She had to recognise a life where she had made a promise to look after her sister 'for ever'. In that life, it had been appropriate that she should care for her, then child, sister. They were very close, soulmates even. But it was not appropriate in the present life. After she redefined the vow, her sister was able to go into treatment for her alcohol problems. My client found herself pregnant with a soul she knew had been waiting to come: 'He is part of my soul,' she declared.

Equally, we may have been with someone for many incarnations and now have decided on a change, but we forget once we are in incarnation. We yearn for the perfect love we know we have had before, the soulmate who must be out there. We get pulled back together, only to find we lose them. We have to let go of the past.

I once counselled a woman who had been in a soulmate relationship for years, but had been unable to live with her lover because he was married. Eventually he left his wife and obtained a divorce. They were 'blissfully happy'. A Pisces, the zodiac sign that yearns for total union with the beloved, her only gripe was that she knew they could merge, become one, and he was resisting fiercely. Six weeks after she was able to marry her soulmate, he died. Deeply shocked, she was worried that it was a punishment for having taken him away from his wife. She was contemplating suicide because she felt so strongly that they were meant to be together. He then came to tell her that it would not have been possible for either of them to develop as they had to if they had stayed together. He had to go on, he could not merge and become one with her as she so longed for him to do. She, on the other hand, had her own pathway to follow. One day they would be reunited, but not until she had completed her own karmic purpose.

Cleaving to what is akin

Those who are halves of a male whole pursue males... because they always cleave to what is akin to themselves

—*Plato*[25]

When speaking of soulmates, the assumption is generally made that this is a male-female phenomenon – that the original soul was split between male and female. But this is not how Plato describes it. As we have seen, he is insistent that, in the beginning, there were beings who were wholly male and, therefore, when split became two male halves. Similarly, the female soul became two female parts. It was only the hermaphrodite soul that became one part male and one part female.

Plato is somewhat scathing about these latter souls:

> *Those men who are halves of a being... hermaphrodite, are lovers of women and most adulterers come from this class, as also do women who are mad about men and sexually promiscuous.*[26]

To Plato the ideal is the man who pursues his other, male, half. He says:

> *Such [men] are the best of their generation, because they are the most manly... It is not shamelessness which inspires their behaviour, but high spirit and manliness and virility, which lead them to welcome the society of their own kind... Whenever the lover of [men] – or any other person for that matter – has the good fortune to encounter his own actual other half, affection and kinship and love combine to inspire in him an emotion which is quite overwhelming, and such a pair practically refuse ever to be*

separated even for a moment… No one can suppose that it is mere physical enjoyment which causes the one to take such intense delight in the company of the other. It is clear that the soul of each has some other longing which it cannot express.[27]

Plato could perhaps be accused of bias towards the Greek ideal of his day, but nevertheless, he is making a valid point. There is no reason at all why soulmates, or twin souls, should actually be of a different gender. It is quite clear from regression work to other lives that we all take on not only various roles but also become male or female as appropriate to those roles. So, if we insist on being with our soulmate throughout eternity, we may find that same-sex relationships will become necessary from time to time, or on exploring the past, we may find that this has always been the chosen path of our soul. We may also well find that, just as with heterosexual couples, we have chosen to incarnate with our soulmate to support, or be supported by, someone we love at a deep soul level. On the other hand, it may simply not matter to us what sex our partner is. What may matter is that we learn to relate intimately.

I have undertaken a considerable amount of regression and astrological investigation for both gay and lesbian relationships. In my experience, there is no one answer. Plato's theory may well be correct: that there were three 'sexes' and this has been continued on. Certainly, one of my gay friends is convinced that sexuality is a continuum not an either/or choice. He sees people as tending towards the middle, heterosexual, or towards either end, homosexual, but with the possibility for moving anywhere along the spectrum.

What has emerged during regressions, and especially those to the planning stage in the between-life state, are various scenarios according to the lessons being worked on. For some, same-sex relationships have been a positive choice – and this often includes people who become HIV positive and may go on to develop full blown Aids. These can be some of the most caring soulmate relationships experienced today. Souls choosing same-sex orientation want to experience, or to go on experiencing, relationships which are not the conventional male-female union and which bring out a different side of themselves. Sometimes they are choosing to develop their feminine or masculine side, so that they can integrate this into their whole being. At other times, they want to explore the aggressiveness of same sex male relationships and channel that energy in a new way, or find a new outlet for the nurturing side of female union. For others, where there is little planning, same-sex relationships may be a repeating pattern: there have been many cultures other than the Greek which saw homosexuality as ideal rather than deviant behaviour.

In other cases, where someone has been, say, female for several lives, they may decide to experience life in a male body – quite often to break out of a soulmate deadlock they find themselves in. That choice may be forgotten when in incarnation and they find themselves pulled towards an old soulmate. The soulmate may retain the previous gender. On the other hand, they may find themselves unable to make the switch in internal gender. This happened to one client of mine. She saw herself as a young gay man. Her apparently conventional relationships with men were actually based on her inward perception rather than her outward gender. In regression, she had been a gay man many times. So, despite the fact that the soulmate she was seeking would have an appropriate body to supposedly complement her own female body, she knew that inwardly she would still be in the same kind of homosexual relationship as she had enjoyed before. She was not changing her way of relating despite having changed gender.

Souls may also choose a homosexual orientation in order to experience rejection, isolation and humiliation. In other words, being the outsider who is cut off from soulmate union. Not necessarily as a masochistic action (although there have been cases where souls believed they needed punishing and this was the way it would be achieved), but as a way of empathising with others in the same situation. From the perspective of earth, it is impossible to judge why people choose such incarnations, but, when in the between-life state, the rationale always make sense and the life reflects the choice made.

Hands Across Time

We loved sir – used to meet
How sad and bad and mad it was –
But then, how it was sweet!

—Elizabeth Barrett Browning

Being so involved in karmic work, I naturally meet many people who feel that their soulmate is part of their spiritual evolution. Patricia is someone with whom I have worked on a long-term basis, both as colleagues and in our individual therapy needs, an association that we both feel goes way into the past. In our past-life work for her, we tried several times to look into her relationship with her partner, but each time we seemed to be blocked. We knew from the glimpses we had had, and from their own individual intuitions, that it was an extremely old connection and one that was spiritually very deep. She had felt from their first meeting that it was a reconnection rather than a fresh contact. They both knew that they had a life-task to do together, but somehow it was not working out quite as they expected. There was 'something in the way'.

They had met each other fifteen years earlier when skiing. There was a strong attraction right from the start:

John tried to get me to make love – I wouldn't as I was married. When home, he came to visit me one weekend armed with a box of Thornton's chocolates (my favourites). The first time we made love it was on the floor in the lounge because it was quite urgent. There was not a lot of foreplay. It was too forceful for me to enjoy it as I was menopausal and very dry. By the end of the weekend, I was quite sore! It wasn't gentle sex, it had an urgency. I then moved in with him and, when we had more time it was much better. BUT – he woke up with a hard-on and I'm useless in the morning. I'm more arousable at night and he goes straight to sleep, so it has always been difficult unless we wake up during the night, then it's great. He's very patient and does all the right things but I've always felt a bit innocent in lovemaking.

Somehow despite the sexual difficulties they felt they just had to be together. As the years went by, however, things got much worse in that one area of their life. Their lovemaking became much more infrequent and eventually stopped altogether:

When we talked about it, we both agreed we love one another very much. Neither of us can imagine living with anyone else. In every other area of life we are really good together: attitude, humour, sport, responsibility, etc. He says he's no longer attracted to me sexually. We still share the same bed and nowadays we have cuddles. There was a time when he wanted separate beds and us to live separate love lives. But I said: 'No way, not for me.' If he wanted to find someone else – fine, but I'll not be here. So, we plod on and he is changing greatly, so I continue to hope!

This was when she came to see me. We did several sessions but just could not seem to get to the root of the matter. Then she did a tie cutting session with him during a workshop:

I can see a large twisted penis going into my vagina. I dont know what to do. I can't release it. I think it's me that is holding on. I am [sitting cross legged on the floor and find myself] rubbing myself on my heel and becoming sexually aroused. I realise I need to have an orgasm to release it. As I become more aroused it slides out with the fluid, no longer twisted. It goes back to John and at this point it is normal, so I dont need to cut it off! Then I feel the unconditional love that is already there between us.

This was in the morning session. It seemed that she needed to release that tie before she was able to see what had created it. In the afternoon she went into a past-life regression specifically to find the source of the problem:

I can see a gargoyle. It is a church. I am wearing a white Guinevere-type dress, low cut, long sleeves, long skirt. I have a headdress with flowing net on its top.

John is coming. It's a wedding; we walk down the aisle together towards the priest. There are pews on either side and a stained glass window. We are walking to the front to be married.

Now I'm in a bedroom, looking out of the window. It's still daylight. I can see the field and the cows. My hands are sweating. I'm terrified because I'm a virgin and I dont know what is going to happen to me.

Watching her, it was apparent that her breathing and her heart rate had quickened, although outwardly she was calm. She was looking out from under her eyelids (what I call the Princess Diana look). It was clear she was an innocent young girl who was very, very anxious about what was going to happen.

I can't turn my head. I dont want to look. He comes and leads me to the bed. It's a big fourposter in a large room with two windows with heavy damask drapes. It has panelling and a fireplace.

Here she becomes really agitated. It is clear she is looking around the room, anything rather than look at him:

I'm feeling very panicked. I dont want to look…Aaargh…

Piercing, heartrending screams tear through her. She starts pulling at her hair and biting on her fist. Afterwards she said that there was no foreplay at all. He was ignorant of what to do, as she was, so he just penetrated her without warning. She had bitten her fist to kill the pain and stop her screams. Then:

Now he's withdrawn. I'm bleeding. He's gone to the chair in the corner near the window. He's sobbing, head in his hands. I go to kneel in front of him and take his hands. We love each other so much. We make a vow never to make love again because he loves me so much and does not ever want to hurt me again. After this we sleep in separate rooms. There is great love between us, but we dont express it physically.

I took her forward to her death to see if this changed:

I can see myself on the bed. I'm dying. It's the same bed, the same room. He is sitting in the corner, an old man. There is still great love between us, but we never made love again after that first time.

I asked her to reframe the original scene (one of the ways past-life healing can be effected), so that we could change the outcome and release the vow because, as she said, 'It's not right, it shouldn't be like this.'

> 'This time we play gently and take our time. When I am ready, he enters me with no problem and no pain, only pleasure and great joy.
> [The sounds this time were of ecstacy.]

After the reframing, she went back to her death again:

> As I die and go to the afterlife, he joins me and we intertwine and move up and up into the light, to quite a high level. I think: 'This marriage is made in heaven' and feel great emotion. [sobbing and smiling at the same time] Great joy, great sorrow. This is true union. We are united at a higher level which always remains. I can see the work we have to do together, and the place where this will take place. I know it will be'.

As she went through this latter part her face was blissful, even when she was sobbing: it was tears of joy rather than pain. As she intertwined with him, she was reaching up to the light. The vow was dissolved, the old pain forgotten.

Interestingly enough, they were just about to set off on a round-the-world trip. The first stop was to be Bali. She planned to tell him about the regression before they set off and to play the tape to him. Then, if he felt it appropriate, he too could reframe that vow. She has high hopes of a honeymoon in Bali!

Knowing her story, as the regression unfolded I found it fascinating how many facets of that story had also been present in their first sexual encounter in this present life. I was also very aware of the power of that vow they made out of deep love, and knew that it had to revoked before they could find true fulfilment in their life now. It was clear that here were two kindred spirits who had found themselves so caught up in the past that they simply could not break through. But something had held them together despite this. The great love they had then had in a way been the cause of the problem, but it was also what offered them the possibility of healing it now.

Kindred Spirits

If thou must love me, let it be for naught
Except for love's sake only

—Elizabeth Barrett Browning

When I first began to look at soulmates, I felt I needed to identify what made a soulmate relationship work. I had so many stories of painful meetings, unfinished business and tangled webs that I needed to talk to people who were in relationships that felt right and good. I wanted to differentiate between the difficult-but-still-together interaction of the 'Hands Across Time' saga we have just looked at, and the growing-together-happily scenario. So I spoke to Kate, an actress who seemed – certainly from outside the relationship – to belong to the latter group:

My husband, Anthony, and I have been together for seven and a half years. Our coming together was an incredible leap of faith as I had just got married and Anthony had just bought a flat with his partner. Our lives were set in one direction and with great struggle and pain and shock we realised we had a different journey to take together.

We were not propelled out of our previous relationships by lust but by kinship, a recognition of the other that went beyond words. A strong spiritual glue seemed to bond us together, for at any time in the early stages we could have abandoned the other in favour of the safety and familiarity we had with our ex-partners. But after our meeting we knew things could never go back to how they were, and our lives continue to be gently nudged forward.

This forward motion of growth and change is the cornerstone of the workings of our relationship today. Each of us provides the safety net for the other, enabling us to try new ventures unfettered by the other, but supported nonetheless. It is important to us that neither interferes in the other's individual work, but creative inspiration is always welcomed and received. The reading we had at our wedding from The Prophet *encapsulates the way of being in relationship that works for us:*

> Give your hearts, but not into each other's keeping.
> For only the hand of Life can contain your hearts.
> And stand together yet not too near together:
> For the pillars of the temple stand apart,
> And the oak tree and the cypress grow
> Not in each other's shadow[28]

The life Anthony and I share flourishes through the many creative theatrical and writing projects we have together. It is a great joy for both of us to act together and to flow with ideas for screenplays and novels. Some friends can't understand how we manage to work together frequently and not 'fall out'. We answer that our creativity is vital to nurturing our love. We receive so much joy in discovering and sharing the other's gifts and talents. The times we 'fall out' occur during our periods of non-creativity.

In all of the satisfying family or personal relationships I have there is communication on a soul deep level, a reciprocal recognition of that person's essence. So this feeling has not been solely limited to my partnership with Anthony, but with him more than anyone else there is no desire to hide. We are unafraid to show and express our true colours to the other. There is a rainbow connection between us which was captured on our favourite wedding photo.

The freedom just to 'be' with the other means we enjoy a lot of time playfully bonding. Each day, when possible, we have an afternoon snuggle and doze. We make contact — check the other is okay.

The question of whether or not we are soulmates could make us complacent or burden us with false expectations, so we tend to shy away from such labels. For my partner and myself to be together is an unexpected joyful miracle. We have our challenges, but we face them together. There is an ebb and flow of love between us that brings creative fulfilment and fun. It can't be analysed, it just is. To be together is enough.

I also spoke to two people who, to all the world, seem to be soulmates. Everyone who knows them says they have the perfect relationship. They are extremely loving and supportive of each other without being co-dependent and symbiotic. Bianca had said when I first mentioned soulmates: 'I know Jack is only here on earth now because I asked him to be with me this time round.' So, my question: 'What makes you soulmates, why does your relationship work so well?' produced a surprising response:

I had found it incredibly difficult to write or even speak into the tape about Soul Mates. It is only now, having just done an automatic writing session that I understand why that has been the case.

I was assuming that Jack and I were soulmates. Wrong. We do get on extraordinarily well, but that is from much practice in many different places, on many different missions and in many different times.

It is my understanding that soulmates come from the same soul group. Jack and I do not. We come from similar and complimentary soul groups but if looked at from an Earthly point of view, very far apart. It seems that it would be a waste as it were of the group's resources to double up souls in one situation, being that it is a group's goal to gain as many and varied experiences as possible. It is rare for two souls from the same group to incarnate together. Only when there is a particularly tricky situation to overcome and extra understanding and support is required, does that happen. It seems that is not the case where we are concerned.

I have in the past thought of Jack as a soulmate, and perhaps in a way he is. He is my buddy, but from a different soul group. These groups seem to get together and interact for mutual benefit, creating greater understanding over a wider area. In our case I suppose, having done many jobs together, we have an easy relationship that makes many people uncomfortable and sometimes jealous, but we are able to do a good job supporting each other now in this life.

I do really believe that it was only because I asked him to come and help me that Jack is here now. You would understand if you knew him!

All this sounds rather pompous, I am afraid, but there we are; that is obviously one of the traits of my group. Also, of course, all of this is only my group's understanding from their (our) current place in the evolutionary scale. No doubt it will all change as more information comes in. Slipperly lot, eh? You can never take anything as fact.

Looking back on the coincidences in our lives and all the people we know in common, it is fairly obvious in hindsight that Jack and I laid down many situations that would bring us together one way or another. I am glad we both had not closed down so much that we failed to take notice of the signs!

Several times during the writing of this book, I encountered people who have had to radically review their concept of soulmates in the light of their experiences. It was often a case of assuming they knew what soulmates were, and then looking at the evidence of their lives and finding it was something different. But Bianca was the only person who, on looking deeply into the matter, actually reached back to the original soul group and found that, contrary to expectation, she and Jack came from different groups. However, they have clearly travelled a path together over many lifetimes: they are truly kindred spirits.

Miracles do happen

*'Whatever you choose to do, trust your passion; it will awaken
your creativity, keep you in touch with your divine purpose
and help you to feel alive'*
—*David Lawson*[29]

Just under a year ago my literary agent Susan Mears and I were heading for a meeting with my publishers, Thierry and Karin Bogliolo of Findhorn Press, whom I had never met but to whom I was due to deliver a manuscript. On the way, Susan suggested we should meet up with two more of her authors, Justin Carson and David Lawson. She thought we'd have things of mutual interest to discuss. It was clear from that brief meeting that they were special people and we kept in touch. I asked them to contribute to this book because I felt that their story, from the little I knew of it, would be interesting. It was, however, only quite literally, in the closing hours of writing this book that I finally learned the full story and realised just how extraordinary it is:

David:

I first met Justin in my sleep, and although I would never have described him as the man of my dreams, the reality of our relationship has been infinitely better than any dream could even aspire to be. My first conscious impression of Justin was the feeling that I woke up with on a summer's morning in 1987. That feeling was warmer and more golden than the August sunshine that was squeezing its way through the blind that covered my bedroom window. A new light was dawning from within me too and gently filtering into my conscious mind as I opened and then slightly shielded my eyes from the brightness of the day. I knew that I had met him. I had contacted the man that I had been planning to meet and, on some subtle level, we had discussed the possibility of sharing our future. I did not have any tangible idea of what this person was going to look like when we finally physically met, nor did I remember the specifics of what we had discussed but I

*knew, without a shadow of a doubt, that I had met him. The feeling
was too strong to ignore.*

*We had a number of similar meetings during that August and
into early September. There were more mornings of waking up with
that special feeling and with a sense that this man and I were forging
some unique spiritual contract between us. If I had consciously known
what was contained within the small print of that spiritual contract, I
perhaps would have been both more fearful and more excited about
the roller–coaster ride that was to come. My relationship with Justin
has been the most positive, thrilling, growthful, challenging and terrifying
relationship of my entire life! I have nursed him through three major
illnesses, sitting alone in a hospital room on more than one occasion
waiting for him to return from an operating theatre and doing deals
with God in the hope that he would return to me alive and well. I
have moved through years of believing that, whatever happened, he
would always make a miraculous recovery, to a year when I really did
think that he was going to die, and began to prepare myself for that
eventuality, searching inside myself for the grace and willingness to let
go if Justin most needed to leave. Just when I had found those inner
resources and was ready to surrender, Justin's recovery was the most
profound and the most miraculous of all.*

*Throughout this, Justin and I have created and led a series of
successful personal development courses that have touched the lives of
numerous people from around the world, travelled to a number of
beautiful and exotic locations, enjoyed the game of life and shared
everything from food to our highest, brightest secrets. Along the way, I
have discovered that highest, brightest secrets are much more interesting
than deepest, darkest thoughts!*

Justin:

*I have to say that the concept of looking for a soulmate is curious if not
slightly spurious. I have heard it said that life is what happens while
you are making other plans, and I suspect that the same thing applies
when establishing a relationship. If you spend all your time looking for
it, it will probably recede further and further into the distance. It is
obviously appropriate to prepare yourself both spiritually and
emotionally, but you probably cannot plan for it or look for it.*

*In my case my preparation for finding my relationship consisted of
doing affirmations related to what I wanted to create for myself in my*

life and forgiveness, both of myself and past relationships, so that in a sense when the next one was imminent, I was ready for it.

David:

I did not plan to meet a soulmate as such, but I was actively planning to attract my ideal partner and create my ideal loving relationship for some months before Justin and I found each other. Indeed in our own ways, we were both consciously planning for a relationship and using positive thought techniques to make ourselves magnetic and available for the right person to come into our lives. A friend had told me that a true soulmate was someone who embodied the other half of our own soul and that if we met this person, we would feel so complete that we would lose all incentive to follow our own spiritual purpose and we would forget about our greatest spiritual potential. He had said that most people who formed close spiritual relationships actually did so with a person who was similar to their soul twin. This connection would be described as being like two pieces of a jigsaw puzzle that were a good fit but did not fit together perfectly. The similarity was close enough to allow for a powerful attraction and create special spiritual opportunities but different enough to allow for the growth and positive transformation that comes with individual purpose. This theory made great sense to me at the time so I set about finding the man who would provide me with an 'almost perfect fit'.

On a regular basis, I sat in meditation and imagined the kind of man that I would like to share my life with. I wanted someone who was as interested in his own personal and spiritual development as I was in mine. I wanted a man who would help me laugh at life and who would support me in the powerful flow of positive thought that I had started to develop over the previous few years. I created a detailed profile that included a clear sense of the impact that I would like my ideal partner to have upon my life and emotions, as well as a list of the qualities that I would like my ideal partner to embody. I realised that preparing the ground for this special union required me to make positive changes within myself, so that my beliefs and behaviour allowed me to be available for it. Love can easily pass us on the street corner if we have not learned how to look for and recognise it and in my experience, recognition of love always comes with a willingness to love ourselves. I created a series of positive affirmations for daily use; I burned old love letters that kept me attached to the past, forgiving my past relationships and releasing myself from old, worn out expectations of how relationships are supposed to be.

Justin:

I had done myself a reading on the I Ching *which had indicated that the best approach I could take would be to concentrate on doing things for other people. This turned out to be very good advice, because not only did it throw me into a whole new world of thought but as it turned out also introduced me to the person who has been my lover for the past nine years.*

I had completed my first ever personal development course. Something called the 'Silva Method' which teaches how to use your thoughts creatively to achieve more of what you want in your life. I found the approach a rather mechanistic one — good if you want to attract a new Ford Fiesta into your life, but less accommodating for some of the more personal and spiritual aspirations of growth. This is not a criticism because having learned some very simple techniques you can either stay there, or as happened in my case, you can use the principles to take yourself forward into whole new areas of life.

A subsequent weekend course showed me some essential hands-on healing techniques and also introduced me to a group of people with whom I set up a healing charity that concentrated on helping people suffering from hiv and aids-related conditions.*

During this time I was using my positive thought techniques to all sorts of ends. My business was going well. I was driving a smart (some would say 'flash') car and I was very happy in my house. But there really was something missing. I had read a wonderful piece of fiction by Armistead Maupin called Tales of the City *in which a character called Mona, proposes something she called 'Mona's Law', which simply stated, suggests that you could have two of the following three: a good job, a great relationship and a wonderful apartment; but according to Mona you couldn't have all three at the same time. Looking back on my life I realised that I had nearly always had two of those three, in different combinations, but I actually had never had all three concurrently, and I realised that I was beginning to adopt the truth of this fiction into a personal reality. A bit like living out a film plot, but I was living out 'Mona's Law'.*

---

* David and Justin prefer the use of *hiv* and *aids* because they feel capitalisation gives too much power to the concept of the disease.

One of the positive thought techniques that I was using is known as visualisation, which I prefer to call 'creative daydreams', where you use your imagination to help you to create a new reality for yourself. Another technique is known as affirmations, which you use to change your basic belief about something. The theory goes that our thoughts help to create our reality and by being creative and positive with our thinking we are more likely to attract to ourselves the desired outcome.

For a period of time I ran a thought along the lines of 'I now create a perfect spiritual, sensual and loving relationship with a beautiful man, for ever'. One of the things I do for a living now is to teach positive thinking and I joke that in the process of developing that 'perfect relationship' I had a series of what I can only described as 'practice runs'. I would meet someone and think: 'Oh, this is IT. I'm in… okay, so I'm not.' And this went on for quite awhile. In one respect it was thoroughly entertaining. I went to a lot of restaurants, mooned, canoodled and all the rest like a puppy only to come down with a 'bump'. Usually within days. To be honest, my relationship record was never very good at the best of times.

I did however continue with my voluntary work. I had effected an introduction to one of the senior hiv specialists at St Stephen's hospital in London and with my new found friends offered our services as God's gift to the healing profession. He thought we were quite mad, but did have the good grace to say that as the medical profession itself had no answers, we would be welcome on the ward as long as we didn't push ourselves on anybody.

This seemed perfectly fair and so we leafleted the ward and were occasionally called in to do healing work, often with some remarkable results.

We then decided that one of the things we could do was to teach people who were hiv positive how to stay healthy. To my mind one of the most damaging aspects of the aids crisis has been the sense that the moment that you receive a positive diagnosis, then you are at the top of the slippery slope towards death, and so we developed a workshop that introduced people to all sorts of alternatives, from herbal remedies to fairly classic positive thought techniques.

I was coming to the point of emotional exhaustion. All this falling in love for two weeks, or even two days, was becoming tremendously draining to the point that I was beginning to say, even to my friends, that if the next one doesn't work then I thought I would give up the idea of having relationships altogether. Of course, in the event, this would probably have been unlikely, but the thought was certainly there!

And then my healing group organised a self-help seminar given by a woman who calls herself an 'Intuitive Diagnostic', named Carolyn Myss. Within her field she is quite famous. Apparently doctors will phone her up from all over the US and say: 'I have a patient in my office who is presenting with a certain condition, but I have no idea what is wrong with them', and she would instinctively have a solution to offer and claims a 95% success rate. Carolyn Myss was giving us a talk on the emotional causes of aids. It was my job to take the donations at the door. I think I even paid it myself. And without knowing what was about to happen, the first thing I ever said to my prospective partner was: 'That'll be £2 please'.

From then on everything happened at tremendous speed. We met on the Sunday and by Thursday he had moved in, my normal sense of caution about these things having completely gone to the wind. In fact it was not unusual for me to loan my house keys fairly quickly to newly acquired friends and I had never been 'ripped off'. I had met people who wanted to use the washing machine, or who didn't have to work for a day or so, and with whom I would leave the keys while I went to work, but this was different. This was definitely 'giving the keys'.

David:

At first glance, Justin was not the person I would have imagined that I would choose to spend my life with. He was charming and attractive, bright and talkative, with an enquiring mind and a flirtatious nature. He appeared to be both the epitome of the social butterfly and the worldly city boy. In contrast, I had imagined someone who was attractive in a different way, someone a little earthier and not quite so pretty. However, when we first met and talked to each other at that healing seminar, I found him extraordinarily compelling. At the end of the seminar, when most people were saying their goodbyes and wending their way homewards, I found myself unable to leave, and at first, I was not sure why. I helped the organisers to clear the room and stack chairs knowing that it would not be right for me to go too soon. Once the room was clear, my sensible reasons for staying behind evaporated, and yet I still could not bring myself to walk back to the underground station and board a train for home. When the charming, compelling man I had met a short time earlier, offered to give me a lift back to north London I accepted, without a moment's thought. I seemed to resolve my immediate inexplicable dilemma, while very soon creating a whole new one.

As we drove, we chatted about the seminar we had just taken part in and about our lives and spiritual development. Justin was particularly engaging, humorous and irreverent. His brightness was seductive and by the time we neared my home I knew that I did not want to get out of the car and lose sight of him. I did not want that brightness to fade from my life. Passionately searching for a reason to keep the conversation going for a few hours longer, I suggested that we park the car and go for a walk. By the end of the walk, I was in love; by the end of the meal that followed the walk, I was convinced that I had found my life partner, and, with a speed that takes my breath away when I think about it, I moved in with him four days later.

Justin:

Although I knew that I knew very quickly, and I know that he knew that he knew, I suspect that David had to test that he knew that I knew and one way for him to do this was that after I had profusely praised his mop of long hair, telling him how attractive I found men with hair of that length, he had it all cut off. I suspect this was to demonstrate to his own satisfaction that it wasn't just his looks that I was most interested in.

I mentioned the use of 'creative daydreams' to attract an event into one's life. Partly, because I rarely have clear pictures when I visualise, I hadn't clearly defined what my 'perfect partner' would precisely look like. This is a good thing because had I described to myself the precise physical attributes, and, for that matter, professional status of my prospective partner, it actually would probably not have looked like David does, not indeed behaved professionally like he did then, although interestingly enough, and this is only coming into my realisation now, as I think about this, his professional abilities and confidence and indeed breadth of experience is currently beginning to resemble to a fairly accurate extent the type of 'match' I had been looking for ten years ago. So in a sense the fulfilment of my original creative daydream is just beginning to catch up on itself after a substantial period of time. Perhaps this demonstrates that the person I found was indeed not only the person I wanted but also the seed of who he would become and *what we will become together, and had it had all arrived packed and wrapped and 'ready to go' we might have missed out on a substantial part of our 'growing together', and indeed might never even have noticed each other in the first place. And the past nine years have most certainly been a growing. We have lived together, worked together and relied on each other.*

David:

Justin and I are very different to each other and yet our spiritual similarities seem to shine out for other people to see. I suspect that it is our similarity of spiritual purpose combined with our obvious intimacy that has prompted many people to ask us if we are brothers. We can walk into a shop or wander through one of our local London street markets and have complete strangers ask us that question. We usually say: 'YES!' and continue on our way. When we began to teach together, pioneering the study course programme in the UK based upon the work of Louise L. Hay, author of You Can Heal Your Life, *we would often find ourselves speaking with one voice. One of us would start a thought, beginning a sentence, and the other one would complete it. Ideas that appeared to land from the ether would arrive in their entirety or in parts to both of us at exactly the same time. Course participants probably saw us as a creature with two heads, one head (Justin) was more likely to keep them entertained and inspired with hilarious anecdotes while the other head (Me) was an endless source of practical healing wisdom and intuition. Our own reality was that both of us could cover the ground that was usually attributed to the other and that when we worked together we would tap into something far greater than our individual talents and gifts.*

From our extraordinary working relationship and the closeness that our personal relationship gave us, we not only created the 'You Can Heal Your Life' study programme together but we also created a series of other courses on prosperity, self-healing, hands-on healing and personal development. We wrote and self-published two small books and three audio tapes. Our courses began to build in momentum, becoming easier and easier to promote. We were engaged in a full-time, live-in, loving, working partnership, twenty-four hours a day. Friends were both delighted and horrified for us. How could any two people spend quite so much time together without driving each other crazy and committing some unspeakable act of violence? In many cases, other people mentally put themselves in our shoes and imagined themselves spending twenty four hours a day with their own husband, wife or life partner and were terrified at the prospect! All I can say is that it worked very well for us. Sure, we had our disagreements about our different approaches to life, but we never fell out about anything else and, in our whole nine years together, I can only remember us having one blazing row.

Four years into our relationship, I had a conversation with a friend of ours about the nature of happiness. He did not believe that ongoing happiness was truly available, moments of happiness perhaps, but not a regular supply, on a daily basis. It was then that I fully realised how gloriously happy I was and how my happiness had constantly increased since Justin and I first met. While I never imagine life and specifically, our emotional responses to life, to be static, I do believe that happiness is most likely to be a regular visitor to the hearts and households of those who do their best to be available for it. If we do not believe in happiness, we do not give it room to move into our lives. However, I also realised that for our relationship to continue to grow, Justin and I would probably get to a point where we would each need to take some time for individual creative pursuits but I did not then know what catalyst would be required to set us on a wider path. When that catalyst arrived, it did not shatter my happiness, but it was shocking and it challenged me to test and re-test everything that I believed in. For both Justin and myself, it stretched our capacity to love and trust each other and it continues to do so.

In April, 1992 Justin was diagnosed with an aids-related cancer behind his palate and he was soon embroiled in a combination of medical and complementary therapies. While we had always been very accepting of other people's illnesses and, within our courses, had advocated a balance between medical and complementary approaches to health care, it had never occurred to us that one of us might get sick. Dealing with the practicalities of continuing to run our business, with the weekly regime of Justin's chemotherapy and our own limiting judgements about healers not being supposed to be anything but gloriously healthy all the time, pushed us both into making new decisions about our lives and relationship. Something had to give and give it did.

Hoping and trusting that this would not be the end of our teaching career, we postponed some courses and I chose to lead others on my own. The workshops that I led without Justin were my own respite from nursing him full time and although I had been a teacher before we met, they also reminded me of the individual qualities that we both bring to the material we teach and that we could still be creative together without always being in the same room at the same time. Together, we were handling the effects of Justin's chemotherapy: fairly constant nausea, rapid hair loss and Justin's marked change of personality from talkative extrovert to quiet, contemplative introvert. At the same time, despite my shock and exhaustion, the need to develop my own creativity became paramount. I needed to feel that my work was developing through this challenging period of our lives. It felt essential for me to engage in something that expressed and enhanced our fundamental health and sanity.

My creativity has always been important to me. Before Justin and I found each other I had been an actor, a performance poet and a writer of small-scale community theatre plays. I had also dabbled in pottery, songwriting, and a number of other creative forms of expression. When Justin became sick my creativity was probably my salvation, that and a strong belief that he would live and get better. I had also held a belief from childhood that I would someday earn a living from writing books. I did not know what kind of books I would write, if anything I assumed that I would write novels, although I also had no sense of when this would occur. Certainly, having a full-time career teaching courses in healing and personal development did not leave space for this aspect of my creativity to develop. However, once Justin had finished his treatment and was convalescing, there was a vacuum in my life and, as you may have heard, the forces of nature abhor a vacuum. Within a short time a mutual acquaintance introduced me to Susan, a wonderfully resourceful and sensitive woman who became my literary agent and very good friend. Susan encouraged me to write a short proposal for an astrology, health and positive thought book that I had dreamed up, and soon afterwards she had found three commercial publishing houses who were keen to produce it. Over the two years that followed, this short proposal grew into Star Healing –Your Sun Sign, Your Health and Your Success. I have since penned four more books about healing, personal growth, shamanism and Egyptian mythology and I am currently writing a book about psychic development.

During this time, Justin emerged from his cancer, like a butterfly from a cocoon. Perhaps he was a butterfly with slightly dented wings, but his spiritual awareness had grown enormously, adding greater emotional depth to the charm and humour he had always possessed. He had discontinued his chemotherapy two–thirds of the way through his treatment and was clearing the toxins from his body using a mixture of dietary techniques, herbal remedies, acupuncture and positive thoughts. We are very fortunate to have a number of wonderful close friends who are also brilliant complementary therapists with their own special knowledge and skills. These friends were, and still are, highly supportive of us and they represented the tip of an iceberg of love and support that we received during that time. Friends, family and clients from around the world were sending us prayers of absent healing, positive thought and light. It is undoubtedly this level of care that has helped us to move beyond the basic impulse to survive our challenges and into a position where we have been able to thrive, expand and grow.

For two and a half years, Justin's health was relatively stable. We began to teach together again, gently at first and with longer breaks between our seasons of courses, but the work that we did became more rounded, more practical and more mature. We rented out our house for a year and divided our time between the UK, Ireland, southern Spain and North America. We did our best to find a balance between breathing a sigh of relief over our good fortune and recognising that many things had changed in our relationship, not the least that we were both living with a degree of fear and confusion about the future. Now, as a healer, I am aware that the healthiest approach to take to life is to realise that while we can make positive plans for our future and make ourselves available for positive experiences, the future is ultimately not ours to control. It is better to keep our attention on the present and do our best to live day to day. However, Justin went through a period of feeling that he had lost his future entirely. His future vision eluded him, and he was unsure about his personal direction. Sometime later, I experienced a similar feeling. It was as if the illusion of being in a long-term stable relationship with all of the assumptions that I had previously luxuriated in no longer applied to my life. Every time we booked a holiday or organised a course or I signed a book contract, I vacillated, fearful of making a wrong move. What if Justin became sick again and I was left to either cancel or complete work commitments on my own while taking care of him at the same time? What if we were travelling and he became sick while we were away? Our natural positive thought suspended rather than abandoned, we both embarked upon an individual journey of acknowledging and coming to terms with some of our deepest fears.

I did sign up more books and we did travel. Indeed, it was while we were wintering for the second time in southern Spain that Justin became seriously ill again. Despite our previous fears, we handled it. Driving ourselves and our belongings back to London, with the help of a friend, we checked Justin into a hospital bed for treatment. Sitting in his hospital room, I plugged my portable computer into the mains and began to write. It was during that period of about eighteen months with Justin first recovering from a toxo-plasmosis lesion on the brain and then dealing with a bout of shingles that I completed most of the work on four books. While it is true that I would prefer to have dealt with a little less during that period, we both found the resources to carry on, craving the indulgence of doctors, nurses, complementary therapists, colleagues and publishers along the way. Fear is always more challenging to deal with than reality.

Justin:

Part of my process of growth has been a serious illness, and we are weathering that together. In my better moments I can see the illness itself as part of my educational process, although I would, frankly, have preferred to have learned my lessons in a different way. However, that has been the way I have learned, and am still learning. It hasn't always been a lot of fun and it has moved our relationship in a way that I wouldn't have expected, and one in which I frankly wasn't prepared for at the beginning, but for which I am truly grateful. I think we know who we are in a slightly different way to when we first met. I think we have an understanding of ourselves, each other and life that we didn't have at the beginning and I am am truly grateful for the process even if some of the challenges we have faced have been more arduous than we would have planned for. One of the areas of our relationship that does not appear to particularly trouble us, although I have seen the choices made here seriously disrupt the relationships of some of my friends over the years, is to do with the financial side of life. The 'who pays for what' aspect of a relationship which somehow simply doesn't matter at the beginning can have serious implications on how it develops. I have been in relationships where this mattered more, and I suspect that it is down to how natural our whole process has been that it has never been a bone of contention, and never particularly troubles us.

There isn't even a sort of barter system where 'I pay for the gas bill and you do the washing up for a month' and I think again that we are lucky never to have made an issue of this. Indeed, I would say that some of the more successful long-term relationships that I know of are ones where the financial doesn't even appear to rate as an issue.

And is David my 'soulmate'? To be honest, I don't know! I do know that life would not be the same without him, indeed I suspect that I might not even be alive without him. One aspect of my healing has in part been the fact, I am sure, that I haven't been ready to leave. He means too much to me to leave behind and I am certainly not ready to be without him. I don't think that I believe in reincarnation in the classic sense. I suspect that it is unlikely that I was ever a slave in Cleopatra's court or an amoeba in some primeval slime, but I am sure that at the end of this life there will be some 'new adventure' to explore – some new learning – and if some part of David was there too, hopefully on some sort of equal footing, then I would be truly blessed.

David:

This morning, in late November 1996, it was the winter sunshine that woke me from my sleep and I remembered the first light that heralded the beginnings of our special relationship, over nine years ago. Justin is currently very healthy and we have an active teaching programme. As a person he has changed from being pretty, charming and attractive to being truly beautiful and wise. He is powerfully charismatic and connected to inner resources that make me marvel with respect and admiration. Our purpose in being together is much bigger than any words that I could use to define it with. We have provided each other with a foundation for our creative and spiritual growth. We have loved and laughed and enjoyed companionship. Our shared journey is growing sweeter, the present more exciting, and the future less important. When you are in love, each present moment is the best time of all. This love story is still work in progress.

For details of books, workshops and audio tapes by Justin Carson and David Lawson, please contact them at Healing Workshops, P.O. Box 1678, London NW5 4EW, UK.

A Love Affair
from another time

I knew you once; but in Paradise
If we meet, I will pass and turn my face

—Robert Browning

So many people have the expectation that their one and only soulmate will make all their dreams come true. But, as we have seen, a soulmate may be here for quite another purpose. Sometimes the soulmate relationship seems to belong to another time that somehow breaks through into present reality from time to time, as the first of these two stories contributed by Sue Boase shows. There could well also be an underlying freedom-commitment dilemma coming forward from the past as the guy is so petrified of settling down, yet cannot break away either:

The lover who fled

Ian first walked into Diana's life thirteen years ago when she was interviewing prospective television presenters. Instantly they got on like a house on fire, exchanging creative ideas and making each other rock with laughter. She employed him immediately. Shortly after their meeting, Diana began a serious relationship with one of her co-directors, even though her relationship with Ian continued to blossom into outrageous flirtatious teasing to the extent that many of her colleagues were convinced they had become lovers. This was not true. Rather, they fired up each other, and together provided unfailing professional and emotional support particularly when Ian confessed to Diana, in private, his bulimic eating disorder.

Diana's romance progressed to marriage, and since her father was unable to make a speech at her wedding due to health problems, Ian willingly stepped into the breach. Shortly after the wedding, Ian moved to America to further his career, where upon he met Celia, an ex-model who suffered from similar eating disorders. Terrified at the responsibility of entering into a steady relationship, Ian returned to England within a short time to set up a production company with Diana. Just as things were beginning to happen, Ian literally took off overnight, back to the States. Diana received a call a few days later to say he had decided to rekindle his relationship with Celia. Slightly put out at his behaviour, Diana continued to work on her own. She finally wrapped up the company to have a baby. Within nine months of giving birth, her husband left her for his secretary, leaving Diana shattered and desolate.

It was shortly after this that Ian arrived back on her doorstep. His relationship was failing, and finding regular work in America had proved much harder than he anticipated. They fell into each other's arms, and, more from the need of comfort than anything, they ended up in bed together. It was then that Ian confessed his 'liking for leather and things like that'. Diana thought little about this, happy to know Ian was back in her life, and they at last were together. Unable to handle this sudden turn of events, Ian, within days, was back in America. He also married Celia, much to Diana's astonishment. Ian and Diana were not to see each other for five years.

Ian eventually returned to England after the collapse of his marriage. He had nowhere to go and was totally broke and jobless. Diana took him in as her lodger. Any feelings for him emotionally or sexually had long gone, but they continued to enjoy a depth of friendship that neither had experienced before. It was then that he confessed to being a cross dresser. Knowing Ian as well as she did and being able to accept him as he was, Diana felt able to support his need to explore this side of his character – which opened up their relationship to even greater depths. During this time, Diana had a short, but intense relationship with Jake, whom Ian did not care for.

As soon as that relationship finished, things became much more intimate between the two. Ian would cook her lavish meals, sensuously feeding her whilst she lay on the sofa. They would also have long detailed talks about their sexual experiences, during which he told her about his sexual problems, and how a woman he'd met had helped him to release his fears of sleeping with a woman while wanting to dress up like one. As these conversations became more intimate, their sexual feelings for each other began to resurface, exploding one night after several bottles of wine.

The following day Ian fell back into his old pattern of panic, but rather than running away, Diana and he decided to talk it through until they felt comfortable again with each other. This lasted for four months. In the meantime, he bought a small weekend cottage in the country, where Diana would visit. It was here that Ian at last allowed her to see him fully dressed up. Even this made no difference to Diana. She actually loved him for who he was, not what he was. They had to face that something really powerful was binding them together. It appeared that now was the time to really discover what it was. They slept together again twice. Ian immediately reacted saying he felt stifled and pressurised. Diana was furious. After all they had been through, she felt she deserved better treatment. She threw him out of the house in a rage and swore never to see him again. A few weeks later Ian called to apologise for his behaviour but concluded by saying he could not go out with her. 'That wasn't her role in his life.' Diana was mortally wounded. She describes it 'As if I had been raped. To be abandoned like that was absolutely horrific.'

Yet the bond was still there, and when Diana began to experience a serious personality clash at work some time later, Ian was one of the people she called to discuss the problem. By this time they had been apart for five months, so they agreed to meet again, and because Diana felt that it could never be the same again between them, she invited him to have dinner with her at home. They talked to the early hours, with Ian full of remorse. However, the evening ended up with them yet again in a passionate embrace. This time, however, Diana refused to sleep with him. They met again three weeks later in a restaurant. Diana making herself look as dowdy and unattractive as possible, but the evening ended with the two of them ardently kissing across the table. Again Diana refused to sleep with him, yet both of them recognised that they were irresistibly drawn to each other. Diana says:

It's totally unexplainable, after all he has done to me and all I know about him, I still love him, and still find him really attractive. It's as if we are an unfinished love affair from another time. When we physically touch, we lock together, and disappear into a different time zone. Then we have to wake up to the reality of who we are in this time zone with all our personality dilemmas and differences.

I believe before we came here, we made a pact to love each other come what may even though I know he can never become the partner I want in this lifetime. I have been his employer, producer, mother, unpaid therapist, landlady, lover and ex-lover and I still want him here. There's no point even trying to explain. It's beyond words. Ian is definitely my soulmate. We will always be there for each other in one way or another.

Diana accepts Ian is unable to offer her anything in the future because, in his words, he's 'so screwed up'. Ian still pulls away, terrified to be drawn into a sexual relationship again, yet Diana is willing to stand beside him as the best friend he has ever had.

The dream lover

Joanna's seven-year marriage ended in divorce when she was thirty. Although the couple had got on well enough, there had been no 'spark' as she put it. She realised that they had grown far enough apart for there to be no reconciliation, and rather than flog a dead horse, she instigated the separation, excited at the prospect of meeting Mr Right at last.

Over the ensuing years, Joanna embarked on courtships with a number of eligible men, none of whom really clicked with her vision of what her ideal soulmate should be. Joanna became more and more disillusioned with her search for her ideal mate, and finally had to come to terms with the fact that perhaps this elusive Mr Right did not actually exist and she was destined to be on her own for the rest of her life. A truly terrifying realisation which pushed her into bleak despair. This became increasingly intensified as she turned 40. At the time she was travelling alone around Central America. A landmark in anyone's life, she spent her birthday night in a broken down hotel, numb with grief. On returning home to England, she made the choice to move to the South Coast – and begin again.

The first year was a challenging mixture of finding her feet, establishing herself in work, and meeting new people which took the edge off her loneliness. Yet as the months passed Joanna began to realise that most of the people she was meeting were either single women, firmly established couples or gay men. Nevertheless, through this new-found family of friends, she began to feel a sense of belonging and support which enabled her to deal more positively with her situation. Slowly the crippling feelings of middle-aged loneliness turned into much more manageable and tangible feelings of aloneness, and for the first time in her life, Joanna began to enjoy her own company.

It was during this transition period that she began to dream of a mysterious dream lover. These dreams occurred night after night, becoming more acute as the weeks went on, until one morning she woke with the overwhelming desire to completely redecorate her bedroom. She literally became like a woman possessed. Previously her taste had leant towards plain, muted colours, but now she found herself drawn to dreamy white muslin curtain material covered with glittering golden stars, which she made and hung. This was something of a first too since handicraft had never been one of her stronger points. She then became obsessed with the idea of buying a new duvet cover and pillowcases which had to be covered with bright pink roses. She also became addicted to the smell of rose and jasmine to the extent that she began spraying her bed with their scent and bathing in the oils. She also spent a small fortune on new slinky underwear. Something was definitely up!

Joanna became filled with delicious unexplained feelings of anticipation at some moments, while at others she would find herself gazing into space, lost in a romantic dream. She became convinced that someone special was coming into her life. But how and when? A month went by with this knowing growing stronger by the day, yet nothing outwardly manifesting; until out of the blue an old work colleague rang to invite her to a birthday party. On the night of the party, while she was changing to go out, a voice inside told her that she would meet the person she had been waiting for that evening. Her immediate response was to tell herself not to be so silly. Yet she knew it was true.

Although it was dark by the time she arrived, due to the warm autumn evening, the guests had gathered in the garden. Joanna walked up to her host to say hello; whereupon he took hold of her and swept her directly into the arms of a friend who was standing on his own under a large maple tree. They took one look at each other and the magic happened.

It turned out that Peter had also been on his own for many years, hiding his loneliness under a mountain of work pressures. Several months previously he too had begun to feel that someone was coming into his life to the extent that he told a number of friends that he was thinking about getting married!

Peter and Joanna embarked on a powerfully healing relationship in which they both learnt to love and trust again. Yet, as time progressed, they reluctantly realised that, although they were extremely close, they were not destined for each other as life partners. Somehow they knew that they had been brought together to help each other overcome their loneliness and disappointment, and once that had happened they would go their separate ways. They parted the best of friends. A year later Joanna met the person with whom she now lives. However, she and Peter are in regular contact and enjoy a warmth and depth of understanding that neither has experienced with any other partner. They believe that they are true soulmates because they accept and know one another on an intensely intimate level, and accept unquestioningly that they are there for each other for the rest of their lives no matter what.

Joanna's need for 'perfect love' was clearly a love theme she carried with her. The search for 'Mr One and Only' so often precludes other relationships from growing. In attracting her dream lover, Joanna manifested exactly what she thought she needed. But, as she found out, whilst he was instrumental in her healing, he was still not Mr Right.

Eternal Triangles

I know we both agreed that if we ever felt the need
to explore some karmic debt with a person that we met
That we could sleep with them
If there were dreams that we could lead with them
Then we could sleep with them

—Julie Felix [30]

Perhaps one of the most painful soulmate experiences is that of the eternal triangle. There are many stories and myths about this ubiquitous experience. Cleopatra, Mark Antony and his wife Octavia played out the tale at the Roman and Egyptian Courts. Arthur, Guinevere and Lancelot repeated the drama in the Court of Camelot – Charles, Diana and Camilla at the modern Court of St James. Many people play it out in their everyday lives.

The triangle situation can carry over from past lives and, as we shall see, the participants may well change their sexual gender as the triangle forms and reforms, but the basic story remains the same. In this first triangle tale, the three people concerned came back into the present life as women and became involved in a complex lesbian relationship:

Suzanne and I had been lovers for nearly two years. After three failed relationships, disillusionment had set in, and I felt emotionally weary. Consequently I welcomed Suzanne's decisive nature. It seemed natural to follow her saturnian lead. She had definite ideas about everything. She was upset if I read at the breakfast table, saying this was bad manners. She would make appointments with me if there was something we needed to talk about. She took my fading career in hand with real success, and when she decided we should go on a peace march, she supervised the purchasing of the proper rucksack, sleeping bag, and all other appropriate equipment.

For several years I had spent two weeks in May on the island of Lesbos where I participated in an intensive yoga course. Whatever relationship I was in, I had decided this was my solo time where I could share with other yoga participants, but not be entangled in personal interaction. When Suzanne suggested she join me after I had been there for ten days, I was hesitant, but then agreed. It was during the ten days before Suzanne arrived that I met Lisbet.

Lisbet and I both felt the strong link between us, but I knew I was playing with fire since Suzanne was due to come out in a few days. Lisbet is quite psychic and recognised that she and I were soulmates. When Suzanne arrived, I tried to act as if everything was normal, but, of course, it was not. I spent time with her, and yet it seemed my spirit was with Lisbet. I finally had to own up, admitting my attraction to Lisbet, but explaining that it was merely an attraction, and that I wished to continue my relationship with her. I certainly wasn't prepared for what followed. Suzanne completely freaked out and proceeded to punish me with the dedication of the 'wicked witch' in a fairy tale.

Lisbet's nature was much more mercurial than saturnian. Her sunny personality was an obvious contrast to that of Suzanne. One night I had a dream that threw an interesting light on the situation. It was a dream that I believe revealed a past life. In this past life I was female, and both Suzanne and Lisbet were male. I don't know when in the past it took place, but it was a Polynesian setting complete with palm trees and moonlit surf.

I was a young girl in what would be the equivalent of a 'respectable family'. Suzanne was a young man whose parents were friends of my parents. A marriage was arranged, and I married Suzanne (in her male form). He was an ambitious young man with strict rules as to what was acceptable and what was not. Lisbet was a young man whom I had grown up with. As children we swam together, climbed trees, and had secret places where we would play and create our own fantasies. He was a fisherman's son, and not considered a candidate for my husband. After my marriage to Suzanne, I became depressed and lonely. Then, eventually, I met this childhood friend (Lisbet) secretly. We would go for moonlight swims and we became lovers. After sometime, my husband (Suzanne) found out about my infidelity. He beat me, called me all kinds of naughty names, and I was forbidden ever to see Lisbet again.

In this life, after several months of attempted reconciliation with Suzanne, we finally decided to separate. Shortly after that, Lisbet and I became lovers. Although we are no longer together, I still consider Lisbet to be my soulmate, my 'brother-sister' throughout eternity. We shall see!

So many people had come to me with this kind of story that I began to feel that something very real was being played out down through the ages. In a meditation I asked where it all began:

Triangles hung in the air. I was told that the event I was to see was the start of many 'eternal triangles'. This event appeared to take place on a planet far from earth. It was a barren place with strange, otherworldly colouring: slate blues and greys, pale sandstone and yellow ochre – like the Egyptian desert at twilight. The beings here were humanlike, but not so solid. They hung ethereal in the air or walked lightly on the earth. Reproduction was by means of binary fission. The being simply split in two (like Plato's soulmates). On sacred occasions, two beings could come together to make a body for a very special soul to incarnate into. This would be a 'holy being'. In other words, sexual union was a sacred act, reserved for a particular purpose. Procreation was a part of everyday life but that everyday life was far from earthlike.

There was some kind of catastrophe. It was hard to tell what happened. Many died. It looked like the devastation after a nuclear explosion; everything was laid to waste. From then on, instead of splitting into two, many of the beings split into three. This created a 'pair' and an 'outsider' who was forever trying to find a place to belong. The pairs would draw together naturally, shutting out the 'outsider'. The outsiders would try to form relationships together, but would always seek to return to their original triangle as this was the only place that felt like home. In this way the 'eternal triangle' was created. I was told that many souls lived this out on earth, with the three souls concerned taking on many different roles and genders in an effort to heal the split.

I assumed that this vision was allegorical rather than actual, but since then several other people have told me of the same vision and their belief that it took place on a planet far from earth. The jury is still out on that as far as I am concerned, but I did find it helpful in picturing why so many people get caught up in the, seemingly, eternal triangle. As far as I can tell, it is not always the original three parts of the one being that are attracted together. One of the three players in a triangle saga may well be an 'outsider' who is trying to find a place to belong – in which case the 'triangle' may form for one life only although the effects can carry over. This can affect the outcome depending on whether the existing partnership is one of soulmates or not. A quite usual scenario in the triangle situation is that two people marry, and then a soulmate of one of them comes along – or the third part of the original being arrives on the scene.

I was working for 'New Age Guru' and energy channeller David Icke at the time I had the triangles picture, attempting to make sense of the relationship between him, his wife Linda, and Mari Shawson – a channeller with whom he had become sexually involved, apparently as part of an earth healing exercise.[31] Both he and Mari had been told, through channelled sources, that they had to use their combined sexual energy as they travelled the world healing important energy sites. David says he resisted this idea at first, out of love for his wife, but was told 'It has already happened on the etheric; it has to happen in the physical'. So he complied.

Naturally the whole episode had caused great distress to Linda, who had had Mari living with them for the best part of a year while the eternal triangle worked its way through and a book *Love Changes Everything* was written. David Icke said the bond between him and Linda had been strengthened by the experience, but that Mari had done all she could to drive a wedge between them. Mari in turn said David had promised her he would leave Linda, that they were soulmates who were destined to live together. Mari had had his baby and then Linda too became pregnant. The whole thing seemed a total karmic mess. Accusations were flying around, which the press were only too happy to pick up. The charts of all three people involved were tightly bound together. Trying to separate them out astrologically was impossible, there were so many soulmate connections across all the charts it was a case of perm any two out of three and you'll find a soulmate.

This was by no means a new phenomena and they were only one of a number of spiritually-connected partnerships who found themselves in the same situation at around the same time (1991-2), quite a few of whom contacted me. In each case, it felt like an ancient contact being renewed, an old pattern closing up. In many it felt like fate. The relationship was torn apart by a third party. Often this third party acted as a catalyst, breaking down the relationship and then moving on, leaving pain and crisis behind but also the possibility of change and growth. Sometimes one of the partners left with the new partner, causing great anguish to the one left behind. Each threesome solved the dilemma in their own way, but for many it was an initiation into a new way of life. The vision I had did little to clarify individual cases, but more information was to come on these triangles.

Astrologer Pat Gillingham was receiving channelled teachings related to what her communicator called 'triad souls'. He told her that there were many threesomes (the triad soul) who had been created long ago. Such threesomes were drawn together down the ages and many were incarnated on earth at the present time because they had specific work to do. The David–Linda–Mari relationship appeared to be one of these triads. As David himself wrote about triangles at important earth energy sites:

> One point of the triangle attracts positive energies, another negative, and the third point harmonizes the two together.
> It has a similar harmonizing role with spiritual and physical energies also.[32]

In physical relationships, occasionally it will happen that the third party brings the other two more into harmony. But this is not always the case. Sometimes the adjustment means that fragmentation occurs. David and Linda remained together after the Mari incident. Mari came into the relationship for a time, played her part, and then left. In many other cases, the original partnership either split totally or the 'extra person' was accommodated into the relationship in some way. In some cases, for instance, they would live as two couples split between two homes, in others they lived together. For some people these threesomes have always existed. I remember reading the story of a woman who lived with identical twins. She simply could not decide between them, loving them equally. They in turn loved her and felt no jealousy between them. They lived together amicably, even sharing a bedroom together.

Pat Gillingham's communicator also told her that the triads were symbolised by the planets Neptune (love), Uranus (will) and Pluto (power). We all have these planetary 'gods' within us and they act out their archetypal dramas, sometimes with our conscious consent, sometimes not. According to Pat's source, the souls, each attuned to a particular planet, were playing out an archetypal love/will/power struggle which had to be resolved. A similar idea is found in esoteric astrology where a soul is aligned to a certain ray, each ruled by a planet. Particular rays interact and have to come into harmony.

From the symbolic picture I had been shown, it appeared that both twin souls and eternal triangles are relevant to relationships at the present time, with many people finding themselves in one role or another. I was told that the twin souls go back to the androgynous beings of early Atlantis and Lemuria that 'split' during catastrophes there. Whether this latter picture was symbolic or not hardly seemed to matter. It was a metaphor for a psychic truth. We are all busy searching 'out there' for what, in the end, must be recognised as a part of our inner being that has been split off, or projected 'out there' onto the outer world and has therefore remained unreachable. We can only find our twin soul, or the three parts of the triangle, in the integration of our own inner energies.

Ancient history

Nevertheless, that archetypal struggle between the different facets of the eternal triangle is one that has been recorded as long as history has existed. In an extremely karmic tale in the Old Testament, one that is still having repercussions today, Abraham was given a vision:

> *The word of the Lord came to Abram in a vision. He said:*
> *'Do not be afraid Abram, I am giving you a very great reward.*

> —*Gen 15:1-4*

Now Abraham did not believe he deserved a reward. He was childless and therefore, under Jewish law of the time, had no standing in the community. (This despite the fact that he clearly led a large and prosperous community.) He was told that his descendants would be as numerous as the stars in the sky, something he could hardly believe. Abraham's wife, Sarah, was barren and suggested that her Egyptian slave-girl, Hagar, become a 'surrogate mother' and a second wife to Abraham. As Hagar then despised Sarah for allowing her to conceive, the story becomes deeply convoluted. Sarah says to Abram:

> *I have been wronged and you must answer for it. It was I who gave my slave-girl into your arms, but since she has known that she is with child, she has despised me. May the Lord see justice done between you and me*
>
> —Gen 16:5

Abraham tells her that her slave-girl is in her hands, 'deal with her as you will'. So Sarah mistreats Hagar and she runs away. An angel finds her and tells Hagar to return to Sarah and submit but promises her descendants will be too many to be counted. As to the child, he says the boy shall be called Ishmael and that 'his hand [shall be] against every man, and every man's hand against him; and he shall live at odds with all his kinsmen'. It appeared that Hagar could not escape her 'fate' and neither could her child (karma passes down through the generations). She had to face up to the karma that came from lying with another woman's husband, even though that woman had herself suggested it. Her son Ishmael, however, although an outcast from Jewish society, became the patriarch from which Moslems claim descent.

Eventually Sarah, despite her advanced years, also bore a son, Isaac. The father of many, and forefather of the Jewish race.

However, this was not the start of this karmic tale by any means. Some years previously, at a time of famine, Abraham and Sarah had journeyed to Egypt. Believing that if the Egyptians knew Sarah was his wife, they would kill him and take her – for she was very beautiful, Abraham said she was his sister. Pharaoh apparently took her to wife – more probably as a concubine. In retribution, 'the Lord struck Pharaoh and his household with 'grave diseases' (Gen.12:17). Somewhat distressed, the Pharaoh asked Abraham why he had lied, and then sent them packing. (Hardly surprising, from a karmic point of view, that the Jews were later taken into so-called slavery in Egypt. If Genesis is to be believed, this is not the only time Abraham lied about Sarah being his sister and let another man take her to save his own skin, but this could well be the same story (Gen 20:2-18) with the details altered as it passed through the oral tradition.)

Nor was the birth of the two sons to Abraham the end of the tale. We can trace the roots of the conflict between the Jews (descended from Sarah's son) and the Moslems (descended from Hagar's son) back to this particular eternal triangle. The story repeats down through the ages as the archetype and collective karma continues to take hold. What happens in the collective, the many, also happens in the personal, the few. Eternal triangles recur throughout the ages.

The disciple was sitting with his guru one day under the banyan tree. The Master asked of his disciple: 'What troubles you my son?'

'Ah! Well might you ask, oh! Master. I feel it is time that I moved on and searched for my beloved soulmate, the one who is to be my perfect partner, the most beautiful woman in the whole Universe.'

So be it my son, but, remember, when all your searching is over, do return here with her.'

'Yes oh! Master, that will surely be.'

Many years later the disciple returned to the Ashram, alone and somewhat disconsolate. When they finally met, the Master welcomed him warmly and enquired of his search, 'Did you find that whom you sought?'

'Beloved Master, yes indeed. I found her of whom I had dreamt. She was indeed the perfection of those dreams, the perfect woman.'

'Well my Son, where is she?'

'Oh! Great sadness, my Master. She was looking for the perfect man!!!'

—All till my youth was gone
A Sufi tale as told by Ron Cuthbertson

A different version of the eternal triangle occurs when someone loves someone who loves someone else. The poet Willam Butler Yeats suffered from unrequited love for well over twenty years. In a highly complex relationship, a triangle wove its way through his life and, 'took his youth.' It was not all bad, however. This was his creative muse, fuelling his greatest works and underpinning his life. The astrology between him and his great love was powerful, perfectly expressing a 'can't live with her, can't live without her' dilemma and the mystic merging that their souls eventually undertook.

The object of his affection, Maud Gonne, steadfastly refused to marry him but remained his close friend and magical colleague.[33] He was sure she was his soulmate. Both remembered past lives together. Maud dreamt that they had been sister and brother sold into slavery. They had been each other's sole support. Throughout Maud's life, she would always turn to Yeats at times of trouble.

On first meeting Maud, Yeats thought her 'a goddess'. He says in his memoirs that he had never seen a woman of such great beauty. She brought about in him 'an overwhelming tumult'. He proposed to her on several occasions, but she always said no. Almost ten years later they underwent a soul marriage. Both had a dream the same night. Yeats dreamt that she kissed him for the first time. Maud dreamt of a 'great spirit' who took her to a throng of spirits, amongst whom was Yeats. He put Yeats' hand into Maud's and said that they were married. When Maud related this dream to Yeats, she told him she could never be his wife in reality because there was someone else. However, commentators have seen this as a time when, if Yeats had pursued his quest, he could well have succeeded (Maud was at that time separated from her French soulmate). But, somehow, he preferred his woman to be unattainable (hardly surprising given their astrological synastry with its strong Uranus–Neptune flavour).

A few days later they did a silent meditation together. Maud found herself 'a great stone statue through which passed flame'. Yeats became 'flame mounting up through and looking out of the eyes of a great stone Minerva'. They both took this to confirm that they had made a spiritual and mental marriage. But once again Maud refused to marry him 'in the flesh', saying that she had an abhorrence of physical contact.

In 1908, almost ten years after their first spiritual joining, when exploring sexual magick on the astral plane (a kind of out-of-the-body tantric sex), they again shared a mutual experience, a 'renewing of their vows'. This followed on from Maud's separation from her husband whom she had married having, as Yeats saw it, forgotten the sacred vow between them. It was an experience that went far beyond the physical and the two do not appear to have been in close proximity at the time. Their second 'mystical marriage' extended over a period of several days. Yeats consciously evoked two red and green globes, a symbol of sexuality, mingling together. He experienced a 'great union' with Maud. On the same night, Maud wrote to him about an experience she had just had. She had assumed a moth-like form, her own body travelling to the astral realms, and focussed on Yeats. He appeared as a great serpent and they travelled somewhere in space. She looked into his eyes and they kissed. They melted into each other until they formed one being – a complete and total union. On reading this, Yeats immediately imaged himself as a great serpent, becoming one with Maud. At the same time, Maud felt him join her, so that they again became one being in ecstasy. Following this experience, Yeats wrote to Maud: 'I think today I could let you marry another... for I know the spiritual union between us will outlive this life, even if we never see each other in this world again.'

When one of his biographers, Richard Ellman, interviewed Yeats' wife (who he had married towards the end of his long involvement with Maud) after his death, she was firmly of the opinion that her husband and Maud Gonne had been lovers in 1908.[34] The question remains, however, as to whether it was a physical or spiritual affair. The magical working had been undertaken separately, but Richard Ellman had found reference to them staying together in France that year and Maud saying she could not continue. Exactly what with was not specified, but it could just as well be with the astral working as with a physical relationship. With both Uranus and Neptune featuring strongly in the aspects between their charts, sexual magick was a natural outlet for the magnetic energies between them. Uranus did not then have to worry about commitment nor Neptune about holding back from being totally absorbed into the other person – for a time. The experiences they had during the magical working were far more powerful than anything that happened to them whilst anchored in the reality of bodily existence.

Maud, a priestess of the Hermetic Order of the Golden Dawn, was a striking figure. Six feet tall with copper coloured hair she was the daughter of a English army officer but became an Irish patriot who campaigned against the British Empire and advocated Home Rule for Ireland. As an aristocratic revolutionary she preached her message with great passion, and incited people to violence at a time, the 1890s, when most women were confined to the home. However, she was also one of the prime movers of the new amnesty movement and had a deep interest in spirituality.

Maud was involved in a thirteen-year long, illicit relationship with a married French politician, Lucien Millevoye, with whom she had an illegitimate child, Georges. Millevoye was, in Maud's eyes, her soulmate. At their first meeting, Maud was sure they had met before. They made a pact, he would help her free Ireland. She would help him win Alsace-Lorraine. Some commentators have felt that Maud, who in her autobiography relates that she had made a pact with the devil to give him her soul in return for freedom to control her own life, might also have included in that pact that he (the devil) would give her Lucien Millevoye. Certainly Maud had a feeling that her soul was lost and that much of the tragedy in her life was due to this pact – her father died ten days after the pact was made.

Maud and Lucien's child died young. Obsessed with keeping in contact with the spirit of her dead child, Maud went to a seance with Yeats. The seer, Moina Mathers, described a sad, dark-eyed lady in grey veils who was attached to Maud. Maud had frequently seen this 'grey lady' when she was a child. Yeats and Maud had performed a magical ritual a few days prior to the seance at which the grey lady appeared. She said she was Maud's *ka* from a former life. The *ka* is an aspect of the personality that survives death and can remain earthbound. It is a kind of 'etheric double' which holds the soul, or spiritual essence, in incarnation and also houses the personality. It lives on independently in the astral world after the physical body dies. In Egyptian thought, it was the unsatisfied desires or unlived impulses of the *ka* that pulled the soul back into incarnation. But the *ka* could also continue its own afterlife when other parts of the soul had reincarnated.

Maud's *ka* told her story. Apparently she had been an Egyptian priestess who came under the influence of a priestly lover and gave false oracles for profit – strictly against the rules. As a consequence, the *ka* had remained 'a half-living shadow'. Yeats, in that life, had befriended the priestess and helped her to escape. Finally, she had died in the desert, but her *ka* remained split off from her soul. Now the priestess wanted to be reunited with Maud.

Moina Mathers felt the 'grey lady' was adversely influencing Maud, who had been almost verging on madness with her grief and blamed herself for being a 'bad mother' and neglecting her child, whom she had left in France (she had to keep the illegitimate birth secret). Maud herself said that when the grey lady appeared at the end of her childhood bed, the apparition confessed to having killed a child and was full of remorse. Moina Mathers confirmed this in her own vision. Maud joined the Golden Dawn the next day so that she could learn to command and control such entities. (It would perhaps have been more appropriate to do a soul retrieval and bring this split-off, shadowy side back into Maud's own self, but this option does not seem to have occurred to Maud or her magical advisers. As it was, the *ka* caused difficulties for Maud throughout her life.)

Maud was determined to reincarnate her child's soul. The Golden Dawn were firm believers in reincarnation and had rituals for rebirth and to 'call a soul forth'.[35] Maud eventually persuaded her unsuspecting lover, Millevoye, to visit the child's grave with her on All Hallow's Eve. This is the time when the veil between the worlds grows thin. Souls can cross. They made love in the memorial chapel vault and she became pregnant once again – and no doubt, was convinced she was carrying the same soul. Her child was a girl. Some time afterwards, the relationship broke up. Eventually, Maud married someone else. When that marriage broke up, Yeats and Maud made their second mystical marriage.

Yeats remained her close friend throughout, although her marriage did release him into his own eventual marriage. But the two remained tied on the soul level. It was to Maud that Yeats wrote:

Others because you did not keep
The deep sworn vow have been friends of mine
The triangle plays out to the end.

Eternal triangles are often formed where someone meets up with two previous soulmates or members of the soul group, in one lifetime. Recognising that it is a soul link helps, but few people are this aware in the beginning. So often one person is happily married, and along comes soulmate number two. At other times, I have known people to leave their (unsatisfactory) marriage for a soulmate, only to find another one comes along almost immediately. As someone said: 'How can I possibly love two men with all my heart and soul at the same time? But I do!' In her case, the lesson was to let go of soulmate number one – who could not leave his wife and family – and drop all her illusions and dreams around him, and to go into a relationship with soulmate number two who was available. When she did this, she finally found the happiness that had been eluding her all her life.

Healing equilibrium

One of the most positive eternal triangle situations I have seen came not in a conventional love relationship – perhaps the reason why it worked out so well. The three women concerned were all heterosexual. One was living with a much younger soulmate with whom she had had quite a difficult passage through to the peaceful place they now found themselves in. Another of the women was still in the process of working on herself; she felt relationships with men could wait until she was in good relationship to herself. The third woman thought she was also in that space, until she met a warm, gentle loving soulmate who taught her a great deal about love.

The three were drawn together through a mutual interest in healing. Within the threesome, they were aware of old issues around power. All remembered having been part of a 'sisterhood' in ancient times. This sisterhood had been destroyed by the efforts of outsiders. Its members had scattered. All three were powerful women in their own right, all were strongly in touch with their masculine energy. When they came together, naturally there were a few explosions as each tried to find her place in the group. There were some strong feelings, jealousies surfaced – not always related to the present life. Passions were aroused, but they felt that they belonged together – were soulmates – and had a job to do so they were determined to work through the problems. They met each one head on, nothing was allowed to be repressed. At the same time, they offered each other unconditional love and a space to simply be. Although each was strongly intuitive, they each had their own particular way of working. Each woman's horoscope was 'ruled' by one of the planets that Pat Gillingham had identified as part of the triad soul. One epitomised love (Neptune), one will (Uranus) and the other power (Pluto). Their challenge was to find a way to integrate these energies for the good of others, rather than fighting amongst themselves.

They evolved a way of working which was loosely tied together and which was directed towards what their patients needed. Although all had strong psychic abilities, the 'Neptune' part of the threesome was particularly good at psychically diagnosing what the soul's 'dis-ease' was. The 'Pluto' woman was an expert at working through the body to release soul trauma. The 'Uranus' part of the triangle worked to heal blockages arising from childhood and was an exceptionally good energy transmitter. So, they would pair up where necessary to combine their talents, and, occasionally, all three would work together to bring energies back into equilibrium. As they worked, their own energies harmonised. Eventually, they had no need to work together at a physical level. Telepathically in contact, each could call on the others as she worked, drawing in whatever energy was required. The sisterhood has been repaired and the karma neutralised. They were told: 'The soul group is being pulled together; 'new' members are coming in all the time. Each one takes her rightful place. Not all the original sisters will come together, but they are in contact on the etheric levels. The healing purpose is being fulfilled.'

Serial Soulmates

Sometimes we meet more than one soulmate.
It all depends on what we have come to do[36]

Early one summer, my phone rang. 'Is that Miss Judy Hall?' drawled a Southern Belle. I could almost believe Scarlett O'Hara was on the other end of the phone, so I will call her Scarlett. It was Scarlett who eventually said that she believed our soulmate is here to teach us the hardest lesson.

During that first call, Scarlett merely told me that she had met her soulmate, but he was dying. A prevous soulmate of hers had already died. Could they come to see me urgently? Gradually over the years that I knew her, Scarlett revealed that this was in fact soulmate number three and that number two had also died. 'I guess I'm stuck in a pattern,' she said somewhat philosophically, 'but it's a pattern I would like to change.'

Scarlett's is a story of serial soulmates, and many other things besides. For the sake of clarity, I have tried to tell it not in the order in which it was revealed to me, but in the actual sequence of events in Scarlett's life. Many of the insights she had, however, were with the benefit of hindsight and, as we shall see, the tale meanders through several soul links as it winds its way to a conclusion. It is a complex and convoluted tale.

When Scarlett was eighteen she moved from a sleepy Southern town, where ladies still wore white gloves and napped in the afternoon on freshly laundered white sheets. Life in the big city was something of a surprise and working in a large insurance office a definite eye-opener.

On day three, the door opened and there, in her words, was the hunk of all hunks. One look and she had all the classic symptoms: pounding heart, wedding bells ringing, base chakra alight. 'Come and live with me,' he said. Being a properly brought up young lady, she waited a week before complying. She knew this was her soulmate, her one and only true love. But she was in for a rude awakening. (Unbenown to her, she carried the 'Love Hurts' scenario in the depth of her being.)

Clark was a promiscuous drug addict who was not about to clean up his act on account of meeting his soulmate. Scarlett came home from work to find the flat full of addicts or, in her opinion much worse, one 'special friend' with whom he had been spending the afternoon in bed. Many times she left, and just as many times she returned. She could not get him out of her system. She 'knew we were meant to be together', a view he continually reinforced by telling her how much he loved – and needed – her. She could see the potential he had and what he might be, 'the pearl in his heart', but she could also see the reality of his situation. Scarlett was not a weak and helpless woman for all her Southern ways. She was shooting up a somewhat ruthless career ladder and holding her own amongst much older and better qualified men. But, in the hands of Clark she was putty. Clark, however, was fast slipping down the spiral of addiction.

One day she finally left 'for good'. She had recognised that there was nothing she could do for her soulmate. For the sake of her own life, she had to get out. Two days later, Clark was dead from an accidental drugs overdose. Scarlett got on a plane to England – a pattern she was to repeat several times. She could not go to the funeral, she was terrified of death.

Five years later she met soulmate number two. This was Rhett Butler incarnate. Devastatingly handsome, debonair, just a touch dangerous: the ideal Southern Gentleman to her Southern Belle. Their first date was a costume ball. Naturally they went as Rhett and Scarlett. A film producer was there. He was shooting a film set in the Old South: 'Would they be extras? They so looked the part. She handled her dress as though she had been born to it.'

(Many years later when I came to do a karmic reading for her, not knowing this, I told her she had had a life in the Confederate South. Her great love had been lost in the Civil War (his body was never found), and she mourned him for the rest of her life. She had vowed to wait for him 'for ever'. 'Oh yes,' she said matter of factly, 'Here he is' and pulled out a photo taken at the costume ball. To clear the connection, I took Scarlett back to her previous life with Rhett and she amended that vow she had made. 'For ever' became 'For this life only'. By making such adjustments back in time, and healing the past, the present life can change and nothing need be carried forward into the next life. When, and if, they met again, they would be starting afresh, not bound by the past promise.)

For the next five years Scarlett handled this relationship a little differently than soulmate number one. Rhett lived at home with his wealthy parents and had no desire to move out. She enjoyed her bachelor apartment. But they saw each other most days and the families were very close (and have remained so). One day they would marry. The only cloud on the horizon was that Rhett was always faintly unwell. Hypochondria everyone thought until one day his mother called to say he was in the hospital with terminal liver cancer and if Scarlett wanted to see him she should come quick. Scarlett hated hospitals. She went once but could not stand it and once again took off for England. When she came back, it was for the funeral.

Here we have to take a digression. Rhett was an adopted son. His parents had waited years for their own child, who was born when his mother was approaching forty. She had yearned for this child all that time, never wavered in her belief that he would come to her. She 'knew his soul'. A pretty child, it soon became apparent that he was not strong. At five years old, he died of liver cancer. His mother told me forty years later that she could not grieve, she was so numb. Part of her shut down then and had not reopened. He was her most beloved child, and now he was gone.

She could not conceive again and so they adopted a young child, Rhett. When she showed me the photos, it was uncanny. The two boys were so similar even she had difficulty telling them apart. They could have been identical twins. 'I was sure my baby had come back to me,' this deeply religious Strict Baptist told me. So, the second loss was almost beyond bearing. It was something she is clearly carrying forward to another life, a soul drama that will draw them back together yet again.

In another twist in the tale, when I visited her all those years later I was given Rhett's room. A sanctuary to her dead son, it was filled with silver framed photos, all beautifully posed. 'Oh yes,' said Scarlett when I commented on them: 'He was always having his picture taken; he seemed to be obsessed with it. He so wanted to be admired. He sent them off to magazines. He really wanted to be a star.'

Later that night, unable to sleep, I was watching late night TV. Suddenly there on the screen was Rhett. I looked from the image on the screen to the photo on top of the TV set. There was no mistaking it. This was the same person. It was a 1930s matinée idol. He died just as his career was taking off. Heavy drinking brought on liver disease. Such diseases can be carried over karmically into the next body, or bodies, that the soul inhabits. Here was a link with both the young child who died and the young man who followed. I shouted for Scarlett to come and see, she too agreed. Here was another aspect of her soulmate.

To return to the main story, Scarlett decided to give soulmates a miss for awhile. She moved to England and married an old friend: 'Definitely not a soulmate, but someone I knew I had had other lives with.' She felt safe, 'as though he had promised to look after me' (a promise verified in a later past-life regression and confirmed by her husband's own spontaneous past-life memories).

Meanwhile Scarlett's sister had had a child. 'I took one look and knew it was Clark (soulmate number one)', Scarlett said. Although living on the other side of the world, she became very close to the child. A major influence in his life, she was the one he turned to when in trouble, the one for whom he expressed his 'very special love'. In the family, it was accepted that these two had a bond that stretched over the miles. They were soul companions.

Some years passed. On the surface Scarlett and her husband were happy. But then Scarlett felt this nagging doubt. Something was missing. Were they simply living out his old promise to look after her? She felt that she had a purpose she was not fulfilling. Was she meant to be with a soulmate? She went to one of the 'Find Your Soulmate' workshops so popular in the States at the time. Five weeks later an old friend phoned: 'A friend of mine is coming to England and I want you to meet him. I just know you two have been together before.'

When she opened the door, Scarlett too knew they had been together. Here was soulmate number three. Ashley was in her words: 'Gorgeous, a real hunk, just like Tom Selleck'. There was just one problem. On their third meeting he told her he had only weeks to live, he had cancer. Later, he told her he was gay and had Aids. This was clearly not to be a sexual union although there was considerable sexual attraction between them. She felt it must be for some other purpose.

That was when she phoned me.

I knew very little about them then, which is the way I prefer to work. She had told me that he was her soulmate and had cancer. I also knew that she had had a previous soulmate who had died. That was all. She said of her meeting with Ashley:

> It was magic, just like the time I met my first soulmate; we felt instantly attracted and each felt we had known one another before. We spoke about reincarnation on our first meeting… [On our third] he told me he feels we have to teach each other some lessons and that we don't have much time. We feel so close to each other he has asked me to be with him when he dies… How can fate be so cruel?

When I compared their horoscopes, there were clear indications that this was a soulmate connection, although an extremely difficult one. Essentially, they were going in opposite directions. Clearly this would not be a lifelong relationship for Scarlett but it was an important contact nonetheless. Obviously there were major karmic lessons to be learned and tasks to be undertaken. The previous contact between them had been symbiotic and manipulative with a powerful mothering energy making itself felt. There was a strong need to 'let go and let God' rather than trying to make things work out how she wanted them.

In her astrological chart, and therefore in herself, Scarlett has an 'emotional black hole' that does not believe there will ever be enough love and therefore manipulates and manoeuvres to get what it so urgently needs, which was why she settled for 'second best' with her husband. This hunger for love can never be satisfied by human love; it has to come from the divine part of ourselves. She had to learn to give love out, trusting that it would come back but not controlling the process. She also had the 'Love Hurts' indicators. It was a huge test of letting go, letting happen what would happen. This was combined in her chart with a challenge for unconditional love that usually manifests first as an idealised and idolised lover who is placed on a pedestal and expected to be superhuman.

When the natural human frailities and fallibilities begin to show themselves, total disillusionment sets in. So often with this aspect, what is seen is the 'pearl at the heart of the person', what they may be rather than what they are now. An idealised picture is presented, illusions abound. In this relationship she was being offered the chance to love and accept someone exactly as they were, no illusion was possible. The planetary energies were saying that she had the opportunity to move out of a pattern of merging into an ideal relationship and go instead into a 'higher level' of relationship. This would help her to develop herself unselfishly and release her from old manipulative patterns. It would also allow her to support Ashley in whatever he needed to do.

A particular issue which surfaced for him was the need to teach others that death could be creative and was not in any case The End – as his family had so long believed. By nature an exuberant, fiery Leo, he somehow came over as a rather passive person, always holding back. He needed to find his own strength. There was a pattern of deferring to other people because of a need to be seen as 'nice'; in other words he was a 'people pleaser'. In regression he went back into a pattern of always allowing other people to dictate to him what he should believe in – especially his father with whom he had been in other lives. He needed to take back the control of his life.

When I read Scarlett and Ashley's past lives together, the strongest one seemed to be in the pioneering days when the wagon trains went out across America. I saw them as a mother and child, the father having died. He was a sickly child but his extremely strong-willed mother kept him alive – it seemed – by sheer willpower aided by some rather nasty tasting herbs. In the end, he was begging to be allowed to die. (When Ashley went back to that life in regression he kept whimpering: 'Please mama, let me go, let me go. I want to die.' She, on the other hand, kept promising to always be there for him, to be strong for him – a promise Scarlett felt called upon to keep in the present life). Born in this present life with the indicator of her karmic purpose in headstrong, pushy Aries, Scarlett commented that, when she had first heard of the cancer, she had been aware of wanting to force him to live. She had run round making appointments for him with everyone she could think of. (One of the reasons she had phoned me was that my partner is an holistic doctor who works with cancer patients and who, interestingly enough, uses Chinese herbs – which can taste absolutely foul). Now that she recognised the pattern, she could work on letting go and allowing Ashley to take responsibility for himself. She had to channel her positive Aries energy into strengthening herself so that she could offer him support rather than doing it for him.

Scarlett decided to leave her husband and follow her soulmate orientated life plan. After all, she had made that promise to be with Ashley when he needed her and she felt she could learn a lot from their relationship however long it lasted. She also felt that she had, unknowingly, failed to keep her promise to Rhett and so in some sense this would be a reparation for that too. She released her husband from the promise he had made to her, and the marriage was ended amicably as she was anxious that no karma attached to that relationship be carried forward.

Ashley and Scarlett went back to the States and Ashley underwent treatment that prolonged his life for three more years. Much of this treatment was experimental or unconventional. As he said, he had nothing to lose and maybe it would help someone else in the future. During this time he was in and out of hospital. Scarlett, who had had such a phobia about hospitals that she could not walk through the doors, stayed with him and nursed him. All those bodily functions that had so disgusted her in the past were dealt with quite naturally and lovingly. She learnt how to give him injections, how to change dressings and perform other intimate tasks. His doctors offered to give him drugs, so that they could have sex together, but neither felt that this was the purpose of the relationship. She said: 'We were as close as we possibly could be, we did not need sex.'

As a Virgo, one of her purposes in being here was to give service and another was to explore 'dis-ease' in all its manifestations. She did all she could to support him in whatever choices he made about his life. They worked through a great deal between them. Everything was said that needed to be said. They went through all the emotions together. They shared every possible feeling. They both felt that all the karma was wiped clean.

Eventually, he became very weak, but he did not want to return to hospital; so Scarlett nursed him at home. One day, he caught hold of her hand. 'I'm so tired' he said, 'Can I go now?' 'You know I am the one person who can't answer that,' she replied, 'but I will be with you all the way whatever you decide.' Later that day, after saying goodbye, he drifted into a coma. She held his hand as he slipped peacefully away. She said he looked radiant, so happy to be moving over to the other side. This time, she laid out the body as he had requested, and arranged that the funeral service be a celebration of his life rather than mourning the past. As she said, 'It was the last service I could do for him and I did it willingly' – a long way indeed for someone to travel who could not bear death.

The last I heard from Scarlett, soulmate number four had just arrived in her life. But, she is certain, this relationship will be different. This one will last. As Scarlett O'Hara would say:

'Tomorrow is another day.'

Dangerous Liaisons

The soulmate experience may well not be the marvellous experience everyone yearns for[37]

She looked like Aphrodite: tall, willowly and blonde – exuding sex and promising passion. Every man on the small Greek island was hot and panting for her. The lust was palpable, it hung in the air. You could almost touch it. She had just been told her soulmate was coming, so she put out 'vibes' to attract him. When a goddess puts out with all her will, it is powerful stuff, nothing can resist. Unfortunately for the lesser mortals around her, she was only interested in *him* – the one and only. Dejected and rejected men fell like flies. Aphrodite is ruthless in pursuit of her passion.

Desperate for her soulmate, when she returned to England, Aphrodite, for we can call her so, met several men who might just be... But no, one by one they too fell away. Then it happened. A friend said: 'I've met this man. I know he's the one for you. Come to dinner and I'll introduce you.'

She stood in the doorway, unable to move. There he was. The archetypal tall dark, handsome and frighteningly intelligent man she had sought for so long. Their eyes met. That was all it took... Later that night, as though in a dream, she heard herself saying: 'Why don't you stay the night?' Inside herself though, a voice whispered: 'Don't do it, you'll live to regret this. Don't you know what he did to you?'

Six weeks later she gave a newspaper interview on 'Love at First Sight'. 'I just knew,' she said, 'I could do nothing else. I had to be with him no matter what it cost. This was my soulmate from way back. We had shared many lives. We are fated to be together.' A typically charming Gemini, he had much in common with Mercury, the adroit messenger of the gods and one of

Aphrodite's many lovers. However, as he was half Finnish and seemed to belong in another myth altogether, we will call him Loki after the northern trickster god.

Six months later there was a white wedding, an enormous turnout of friends and family wishing her well. As she walked up the aisle, that still small voice inside screamed: 'It's not too late, turn around and leave NOW!' As she walked back on her husband's arm, the voice asked: 'What have you done..?'

Apart from one incident on their honeymoon, they were blissfully happy. But the small incident stayed with her. She had gone out onto the balcony and sung 'The Chicken Song' ('Chick, chick, chick, chick, chicken, lay a little egg for me'), complete with actions and clucking noises, to a group of hens in the olive grove below. He had closed the balcony door, shutting her out. Were they really on the same wavelength? She asked this question again sometime later when she cooked a romantic gourmet dinner, dressed only in her sexiest underwear. To which he gravely said: 'Fantasy has no place in marriage.'

All went well for six months. They shared many interests in common, and both believed they had a deep soul connection. They wrote for a 'New Age' magazine on many spiritual and occult topics. Then they joined a meditation group. It was guided by a channelled entity who supposedly communicated through a word processor. She was unimpressed. He took in every word.

Two weeks later the group went off on a weekend together. Aphrodite and Loki were invited up to the room of one of the women, whom we will call Athene. When they got there, it was to find the room set out for two with roses, champagne and candlelight. Aphrodite found herself drinking champagne out of a toothmug. 'Odd', she thought, 'I feel like an intruder here.' The voice inside, which had been quite eloquent over the past months, was strangely silent. Waking later in the night, she found herself alone. Going to the door, she was just in time to see Loki emerging from Athene's room, looking flushed and dishevelled. But, rather than listen to her instincts, she preferred to believe her handsome, wonderful husband when he said he thought he'd heard Athene cry out and had gone to her in case she was in trouble.

As the weeks passed, relations in the marriage suddenly became more and more strained. He was absent much of the time, usually without explanation, and touchy when questioned: 'Don't interrogate me,' he thundered. She complained that she couldn't reach him; he seemed to have switched off from her. Their sex life, which had been passionate and inventive, dwindled away to nothing. Later she found out that the word processor had supposedly channelled that Loki and Athene were true soulmates who were destined to be together, to live and work as one. Athene left her husband and children to be with him. She was due to give a lecture tour in Australia. Loki went along too – but forgot to tell Aphrodite. Ironically the media at that time were promoting Athene as a happy, loving wife and mother: an expert on relationships. A closer look would have revealed her cavorting round Australia with her soulmate, but that would have destroyed her image.

While all this was going on, there was a pressing problem for Aphrodite. Just before all this arose, Aphrodite and Loki had bought a house, for which she paid. They had mortgaged it to his family bank – who had insisted that Aphrodite sign the mortgage too. The mortgage money had been intended to renovate the house. Instead, Loki used it for his Australian trip. Now, the money was due for repayment.

When he returned, he moved out of the house but stored his belongings in the cellar. As Aphrodite said: 'I couldn't be free of him while all these things were festering beneath me.' He also cut off all contact with Athene, who then came to Aphrodite for comfort. But the biggest shock of all came when his family bank demanded from Aphrodite the return of the mortgage money. After all, they said, you are no longer living with a member of the family and he has no money to repay. You will have to sell the house and repay us. We can push this through the courts. Her efforts to contact Loki were to no avail, he had gone to ground. Soon she would be both homeless and penniless.

At this point, Aphrodite had a complete breakdown. The experience had wreaked emotional havoc. All her hopes were shattered. Her dreams for the future gone. She felt totally betrayed. Her so-wonderful soulmate had been exposed as a sham. Physically, emotionally and mentally she was at an all time low. Spiritually, she had nowhere to go. She was suicidal and desperate – and furious. She finally understood: 'Hell hath no fury like a woman scorned.' She was immensely angry: this was primal rage. She plotted to kill him. The anger rebounded into her body. She almost died from the complications of an illness more usual in childhood – which her doctor diagnosed as a psychosomatic disorder. During the high fever which accompanied the illness, she experienced herself as roasting in hell. The devil wielding the pitchfork was, naturally, her husband. The bitter experience propelled her into a three-year therapy. That she emerged from it a new and stronger person was the treasure at the heart of the experience.

When she was in the depths of despair, she asked why it had happened and was shown a vision. In the vision, she was before the witch finders. She was found guilty and burnt as a witch (something she had seen over and over again all through her life). Before being executed, however, she was presented with a bill for her stay in prison, her trial and even her inquisition to exhort a confession. All her assets had been confiscated when she was found guilty, so she did not know how she would pay. Not surprisingly, in the vision the chief witch finder was none other than her husband, Loki. She had cursed him as she died, a curse that brought them back together. She assumed the vision embodied a psychological rather than psychic truth.

Notwithstanding, 'coincidentally', she was asked to do some research work on the witch finders in Scotland. There, on the page before her was a picture of her husband, only it was the chief witch finder for Edinburgh some centuries earlier. Her present life husband had lived most of his life in Edinburgh and had always wanted to take her there for a visit. She, uncharacteristically, had refused. Scotland was the only part of the British Isles to burn its 'witches'. Elsewhere they were hung or drowned – burning was reserved for 'heretics'. 'The bastard did it again,' was her comment. 'Not only did he roast me alive in this life too, but once again he made me pay for the privilege!'

This is not a unique story. So many of my clients have a similar tale to tell. Not all of them come out of it as well as Aphrodite did. Her therapy enabled her to take a long, hard look at her deepest patterns. One of her major lessons was to break her old emotional responses. Love and the emotional games attached to it had ruled her life. She had spent so long searching for her soulmate, and tended to assume that every man with whom she 'fell in lust' was the one. An illusion she had seemed unable to break out of. Now she had to detach from that old emotional reaction and learn to respond in a new way.

When she had finished this emotional transformation work, she did a ritual to contact the goddess Aphrodite. She wanted to heal her relationship with love, to find forgiveness in her heart. (Not exactly one of the goddess Aphrodite's strong points. She was known to murder her rivals.) However, after the ritual, the mortal Aphrodite was able to negotiate a divorce settlement that left her home intact. She also insisted that Loki remove all his belongings, after which she felt free. Possessions and photographs hold the 'vibrations' of the person associated with them. It can sometimes be cleansing to have a ritual burning of such items, or to give them away. Aphrodite certainly found it so when she burnt his love letters and gave his gifts to a charity shop.

Much as she had wanted to kill him, she had also recognised that retaliation would start the karmic round again. Although it was hard, she did not want to carry any karma forward into another life, and so she let go of the past and forgave Loki. In forgiving him, she recognised it was his nature. She could not blame him for that. The god Loki too was an untrustworthy husband, and his mortal counterpart a natural imitator. (After the marriage broke down, she found he had left three other women in similar circumstances. He was a con man *par excellence*.) Once the illusion was shattered, she could not only see him for himself but also recognised her own part in it.

Wanting to clear as much of the past as possible, she invited Athene to dinner. Before the Loki incident, they had been friends. She recognised that Athene had been as deeply hurt as she had. Now she was able to extend forgiveness here as well. She finally exorcised the whole tale by writing a novel. In doing so she found a deep well of creativity within her. One of her projects was so apt, a new way of looking at love and what it would bring, that it found instant success. But, of course, if I identified that, it would reveal who she is. So, we must now draw a veil over Aphrodite.

As we have seen, soulmates come in many shapes and sizes according to what we need to learn in order to grow. Meeting your soulmate is not always a pleasant experience, nor does it necessarily occur within a love relationship, as Julia found out to her cost.

She was appointed as theatre manager to a small group of actors who were working as part of a large exhibition. It was to run for nine months in Europe. On the surface it should have been one of the easiest jobs in the world. There was little to do apart from maintaining the theatre space and making sure the actors performed their routines on time. However, as the months progressed serious personality clashes began to surface. The actors were living, eating and working together twenty-four hours a day, which under any circumstances can become extremely stressful. Scott, the eldest member of the group became particularly troublesome and seemed to enjoy goading his colleagues into utter fury.

In a short space of time, the situation became a potential powder keg. Fur began to fly. One actor walked out without notice, which put extra pressure on the remaining nine. Fingers of blame were pointed at Julia, but she felt powerless to do anything except ride the storm. Things however came to an inevitable head when Scott disappeared for a couple of days feigning illness. By this time Julia had had enough, and on his return she gave him a verbal warning. His reaction to the warning turned their meeting into an extremely ugly scene, where Scott projected all his venom onto her. Julia felt that her personal safety was under threat and sacked him. The next day Scott was accompanied off site by security.

Julia was devastated by what had happened. It was the first time in her life that she had failed on a professional level, but far more painful and terrifying was the realisation that this was the first time she had ever faced absolute hatred from another human being. She described the experience as 'penetrating into the deepest part of my psyche, cutting me open like a knife'. She lost all sense of self-worth, which manifested as deep, black depression. 'I kept seeing the hatred in his eyes when we had our confrontation. I kept thinking he'll come back and get me. I couldn't get over the horror that someone out there really hated me. My immediate reaction was to hate him too, but I quickly realised how fruitless this was. It only made me more unhappy, but I found my feelings about him, and how the whole situation actually happened, very difficult to deal with.'

On returning home, Julia began therapy sessions, which, she says looking back, was the best thing she could have done for herself. 'Although I found it hard to accept in the beginning, I realised through my therapy that Scott actually had been of great service to me. Up until then I had always pretended that everything was okay in life, and dealt with problems by running away from them. I also discovered that I hid my low self-esteem behind an over confident facade, which was why my life never really worked properly and I found it hard to form intimate relationships. Scott, albeit unwittingly, broke through my protective barrier and exposed me. I couldn't run away from what was really going on inside me anymore.' She says he gave her the shove that she really needed. 'Isn't that what soulmates are all about?'

By chance a year ago the two met in the street. 'My heart started pounding when I saw him, but I refused to allow my fear to get the better of me, so I walked up to him and said hello. It was obvious that neither of us wanted to talk, but I noticed that the hatred had gone from his eyes, and as he walked off down the street, I was able to unconditionally wish him well.'

'I will always carry that experience with me, but I truly believe it has made me a better person and much more compassionate with others. I also now have a much clearer understanding of what a soulmate actually is. Previously I believed it could only be 'the one'. Now I believe our soulmates are the people who come into our lives when we need to break through our fears in order to learn a vital lesson. They can be friend or foe depending on our state of mind at the time. This realisation helped me enormously because I let go of waiting for *him* to come dashing into my life on his white charger, and just got on with what was in front of my nose. Subsequently my relationships improved beyond measure. It is strange to think I have Scott to thank for that!' she concluded with a smile.

Spurious Soulmates

Her lips suck forth my soul

—Christopher Marlowe[39]

Delusion can play an enormous part in a soulmate experience. We see what we want to see, especially when it agrees with preconceived notions, or when it supports us in destructive behaviour which is not in our best interests but to which we are addicted – and, more especially, when it might have a past-life component. George, one of my clients, told me the following story when he came for regression some years ago:

I was in a wine bar, having had far too much to drink. I was standing at the bar. Helen came up to me, not the other way round, and started talking. So I suggested we sit down. I found her attractive, but I didn't immediately fall for her. Helen was with a man at the time, although he was at the end of the bar. She also had a boyfriend whom she was sleeping with, but she sat down with me.

I was relating to her a story about how a couple of days previously in another wine bar, I was talking to two teenage girls and for a laugh I pretended to be an extra-terrestrial but told them not to tell the earthlings. I said as part of the act that I had to leave the wine bar because I had a rendezvous with a sky chariot. I would have liked to stay and talk to them some more, but this would have meant giving up the act. I think the teenage girls obviously found it amusing, but they were sufficiently young that a part of them thought it could just be true. Having recounted this story to Helen, she told me that she had come up to me because, from across the room, she had thought I was a teenage punk. This was very flattering to me, being almost middle-aged, to be mistaken for a teenager.

She then asked if I knew what the Inner Circle was. Having been acquainted with esotericism for a long time, I asked if she meant the

Inner Circle of Humanity because I knew that there were people who believed that there was such a thing. Then she became really interested and we got talking more. I gave her the address of an organisation which purported to know about the Inner Circle. She gave me her address. When I sobered up the next morning, I realised I had probably said more than I ought to, so I wrote her a letter telling her not to get in touch with this organisation on her own accord as it was private and saying that if she wanted to know more, she should get in touch with me. Which a day or two later she did. I said we had to have a serious talk. She said, 'I was expecting a letter anyway because I often have intuitions about these things.'

So I went round to her flat, taking a tape of Gurdjieff's music with me. She played music on her guitar and we drank some cider and talked about esotericism. I was falling hard for her by now. (That it didn't happen immediately was an important indicator, but I didn't see it at the time.) I actually felt my base chakra opening while I was talking to her, there was tremendous heat down there.

I asked her out and we went out for another drink. (Later we both realised we were alcoholics and ended up in AA although at separate times.) This time she invited me to spend the night back at her flat, although significantly she did ask if I would like to sleep at her flat though not necessarily with her. So we slept in the same room but in separate beds. In the morning I climbed into bed with her but nothing happened. By now I was convinced I was head over heels in love with her: I felt like it. There is a different feeling when you are in love with someone. I felt she was the one for me – a soulmate.

When I asked her how she had heard of the Inner Circle, she told me that a boyfriend of hers had once started talking in his sleep, crying out: 'A half-empty packet of biscuits will get you through to the Inner Circle.' As my name was part of a well-known biscuit manufacturer's name, and would be found on half a packet of biscuits, I took this as a sign from the cosmos.

The following week was St Valentine's Day. It fell on a Friday. I asked her out then but she said she was already going out. I sent her a valentine card and she sent me one. As I wasn't working that day, I had decided to go to France. However, I felt it would be a bit lonely on Valentine's Day to be all on one's own, so I went round to her flat instead. It turned out that she was meeting other male friends, including her current boyfriend. So we all went down the pub and everyone *went back to her flat afterwards. In the end everyone left except for Helen, her boyfriend and myself. It became apparent that the boyfriend wasn't going to leave, so in the end I left.*

Any sensible person would have left the relationship then. However, I was now completely infatuated with her, and it's human nature to want what you can't get. I fantasised about marrying her and even having children as I still thought she was my soulmate. I continued to see her but the following week she told me she didn't want a relationship and I was getting too emotionally involved, as was her boyfriend for whom it appeared she felt little. She also told me that her sexual fantasies were about women. Despite having been told this, I still continued to see her, usually in some bar or other, even though it was apparent that the relationship was getting nowhere and would get nowhere. By this time she was having an affair with a sixteen-year-old, although she was in her early thirties. One night she was in bed with him, while I tossed about on the sofa suffering torments of jealousy.

Eventually I lost my job and had to move away. Fortunately I was able to move back in with my real soulmate, Gretchen, who had been waiting patiently for me. She was aware of what had happened even though we had been apart. Even so, for years I kept going back to Helen. The attraction was so strong. A year or two later, when I visited her she hinted very strongly that she wanted me to sleep with her. I said, 'If I wasn't committed to Gretchen I would probably take you up on that', and left immediately. Now, I realise that the attraction was that she drank and encouraged me to do so. Gretchen did not like my drinking and I thought that Helen was accepting me for what I was – but then I also thought Helen was my true soulmate. It was only when I sobered up that I wondered what I had found so attractive about her.

George had a past-life regression with me to see why he had no money. This is his memory of the regression some eight years later:

I was regressed to a past life where, as a medieval peasant, I had to follow my lord to the wars in France. We took part in the siege of a castle, following which we massacred all the inhabitants. As a result of this, the lord was able to seize all the treasure contained in the castle. The lord was so grateful for my part in the massacre, that I returned a wealthy man. I was able to have my own manor. However, as all these riches had been bought with human blood, they held no pleasure for me. Whether or not this was historically true, it was a psychological truth and this revelation helped me to change my attitude towards money in my present life. Previously I had regarded it as something 'sinful and unspiritual', now I could begin to enjoy it – and to have much more of it. I realised there was nothing wrong in earning money so long as it was got honestly and not at the expense of other people.

It was in this lifetime that I saw myself married to Helen. Whether this is wishful thinking or not, I don't know. When I told her, she came and held my hand and looked very sympathetic. It is one of the very few moments of tenderness there was between us.

When I contacted George for permission to use his experience in this book, I asked him to look back and tell me what he had learned:

In a book called On Love, *quoting his teacher Gurdjieff, A.R. Orage states that one can determine how a relationship will go by looking at the first five minutes of that relationship. In retrospect, there was no immediate attraction to this woman, she was merely someone to chat to and have a drink with – alcohol was the bond that united us. I recounted to her the story of a deception I had practised on other people, and went on to deceive myself. The attraction developed later and was based on self-delusion and alcohol. Whereas when I met Gretchen, my real soulmate and present partner, within five minutes we were chatting away nineteen to the dozen on subjects which were dear to both our hearts and already it felt like we had known each other for ever. Interestingly enough, Helen phoned me recently. She left a message on my answerphone. When I replayed it, I didn't even recognise her voice.*

As George found out, a spurious soulmate can be a very powerful attraction, especially when it allows you to live your life addicted to some form of escapism. A soulmate can be one such addiction, alcohol another. They both involve self-delusion and a removal from reality. As George's story shows, they are not always blissful experiences, but, from inside the relationship, *they appear to be* so long as it lasts, no matter how the relationship would appear to an outsider.

In another false soulmate experience, Gaynor certainly found a part of her soul group, someone with whom she had had many lives before, but this was a part who, in the present life, simply refused to grow. As Brian Weiss warns, an unwanted soulmate may cause you great anguish because, although they may be available to you, they are not in accord with your soul's purpose.

Gaynor joined a spiritual group. There she met Larry. Instantly attracted, he soon became part of both her business and social life. Within a year or so he was her business partner, as well as her lover. But, despite his protestations of eternal love, he refused to give up a promiscuous lifestyle – even though he made many promises to this effect. Gaynor was deeply hurt by this. She believed that lasting love called for eternal fidelity. The group to which they both belonged set great store by spiritual principles and taught that sexual encounters outside a soulmate relationship were bad for the health of one's soul. Larry, however, whilst paying lip service to the beliefs of the group, followed his own rules. He never really took his spiritual development seriously; pleasure took priority. He used her past-life beliefs, and the fact that the leader of the group had told them they were soulmates to manipulate her if she appeared to be slipping out of his grasp.

Somehow the relationship struggled on for another two years before they parted. But by this time, she relied on him for much of her professional work, so she still saw him frequently. Then, on her birthday, they went out for a meal together and Gaynor had a spontaneous regression to a past life in which she had been very much loved – by Larry, she thought. They had been blissfully happy, true soulmates. At the same time, she was listening to Larry telling her all about the new relationship in his life. She said she felt the recall was so that she would know that she had been totally loved, something she had not had in her present life, and would recognise it again when it came. But Larry? How could he be her soulmate when he treated her so badly? What was she to do?

It did not occur to her that the lesson might well be that they had to separate as lovers, so that she could find that love again but with someone else this time. Nor had it occurred to her that they might have been intended to work together rather than become lovers in the first place. She had a pioneering business which brought help to many women. He had the marketing and financial expertise she needed. By mixing 'love' with business, with its resultant conflict, her business went inevitably downhill. She felt the spontaneous recall was confirmation that Larry was her one and only true soulmate. She took him home with her that night, and the night after... She believed in 'higher guidance' and consulted many mediums, as well as the leader of her spiritual group (who assured her Larry was her one true soulmate). The result was total confusion. Some said he was her soulmate, others that there was another soulmate waiting for her. Some said 'stay', others said 'go'.

During this time, Larry was putting her through hell mentally and emotionally. Spiritually, they were not even close, but financially, she was totally reliant on him. Eventually she just could not take it any longer. She left the relationship and severed the business partnership. Her business soon picked up again and became extremely successful. She realised that her recognition of Larry as the character who loved her so much in her spontaneous regression was just wishful thinking. She saw other, less idealised, contacts with Larry in the past. She began to find a more realistic picture of their interaction.

Soon she was being told that her true soulmate was just around the corner. In the meantime, she met a young man who was very gentle and loving. She knew it was not her soulmate but nevertheless, they got on very well. She contacted me to see what I thought. I encouraged her to go for it. I believed that this could be a healing relationship for her. She did not need the intensity of a 'one and only soulmate' at this stage. She had to lick her wounds and give herself time to recover. A gentle, loving man would help her with this. Sure enough, when she became involved with him it was so. For that short time it was good, and it ended well.

What got in the way of all her relationships though was the desire for perfect love, instantly. First of all the unconscious memory, and then the recall of that wonderful love in the past, nagged in the back of her mind. She was not prepared to settle for less. By now she had one or two candidates in view for the position of chief soulmate, but could not make up her mind. While she dithered, one potential relationship after another slipped away. She was always living in the future, not the now. This was her great lesson in life, but one she was unwilling to grasp hold of. When she eventually began to live in the present moment, she found rewarding friendships and some good companions around her. This, she decided, was what she would settle for until 'the one' came along. In the meantime, she would continue to work on her own spiritual development. That seemed to be as far as she could go at this stage.

As Gaynor found, a spurious soulmate, no matter how close the contact was in the past, coupled with the desire for perfect love can lead to many missed opportunities. Opportunties which, had she progressed with them, could have led to her learning new ways to love. For so long she had tried to fit Larry into what she knew he could be, rather than what he was. It is an enormous lesson to realise that a past-life soulmate may have put on a totally new personality in the present life and therefore be incompatible. Truly unconditional love allows those we love, and have loved, to develop at their own pace in their own way. If this does not accord with our way, then we have to stand placidly aside while they take their own pathway. There is an old esoteric story that says if we hold a bird tightly in our hand, we will kill it. If we let it go and it flies away, it was never ours in the first place, but if it is meant to be with us, given freedom it will return. The same applies to love.

Star-Crossed Lovers

From forth the fatal loins of these two foes
A pair of star-cross'd lovers take their life

—*William Shakespeare*

One of the most painful of soulmate contacts comes when the two people concerned are from different sides of the fence: warring families or cultures. We are all familiar with Shakespeare's tragic tale of *Romeo and Juliet*. Their families held an old enmity, but this did not prevent the two young people from falling in love. Juliet recognises that, while the families feud, it is a doomed love. Their only hope is to move beyond the ancestral pattern. She begs Romeo:

Deny thy father, and refuse thy name;
Or, if thou wilt not, be but sworn my love,
And I'll no longer be a Capulet.

What the enmity did prevent was them living happily ever after. Tragedy inevitably piled upon tragedy as the ancient tale played itself out. The families ended more split than ever; they could not find it in their hearts to be reconciled despite the sacrificial deaths of their young. The curse is continued:

A plague o' both your houses!
They have made worms' meat of me.

It is a tale that has been played out many times over the centuries, both in literature and in real life. In *West Side Story* it is reworked and given a contemporary theme, but tragedy still triumphs. Over the years I have worked with many couples to try to understand what lies behind an attraction that pulled them across cultural and religious lines: Catholic and Protestant, Moslem and Christian, Hindu and Atheist, black and white. In every case (my sample is, of course, biased since these are the people who consult me), the relationship had split the families further apart. Despite the sincere wish and, in many cases, soul purpose of the couples concerned, they could not heal the breach. Each couple felt like soulmates, called across centuries to be reunited. Some defied their families and wed; others succumbed to family pressure and parted.

One such story concerns an English woman and her, younger, Egyptian soulmate. They met whilst she was teaching in Egypt. He was working in what she considered too lowly a capacity in the college. He was highly intelligent and had worked as a professional dancer but little future had been seen in this, so his family had sent him to the college to work as a cleaner while he learnt English.

These two were immediately attracted to each other and would spend considerable time talking together. The astrological connections between their charts were considerable. It was no wonder he felt like her soulmate. She tried to find him a more suitable – in her eyes – job, to improve his prospects. Eventually she invited him to her flat and they quickly became lovers – at her instigation. Egyptian men have little opportunity for sexual relationships with the opposite sex outside marriage. The family still arranges the marriage and has strong customs around a suitable match. An English woman, and an older one at that, had no hope of breaking through this system. She visited his family with him, and 'somehow dropped the hint that we were sleeping together'. Whether she hoped this would present them with a *fait accompli* or not is unclear, but the family reacted predictably. They ordered their son to return home and cut off all contact with her, and arranged his marriage forthwith.

She was heartbroken. He appeared to take things rather more philosophically. After all, this is a culture where love still takes a backseat in marriage arrangements. There are other considerations. Despite everything, she did all she could to continue the relationship. She still tried to find him lucrative work in the hope that he would cut off from his family. She simply could not let go of her soulmate: it was too painful. She recalled many lives together; it was a link that spanned centuries. But, when they had been together before, it had been in a 'more suitable' match. Now, unless she virtually kidnapped him and brought him to England, they had no chance.

She returned to England and came to see me. I suggested she should do a tie cutting visualisation to release the past. In my experience, if a relationship is meant to continue, it will find a more constructive way to do so after a cutting. The cutting does not cut off unconditional love, but it does release expectations both past and present. It sets each person free to be what they have to be now, in this present life. When she drew her circle in which to work, it was clear she was uncertain. As soon as she set out his circle and asked him to step into it, she leapt out of her circle to enfold him in her arms. Sobbing, she simply could not let him go. She was determined to hold onto him. She went back to Egypt.

I saw her some years later and asked how things were going. 'I've had to leave Egypt,' she said. 'I just could not forget him. I still want him. I know he is my soulmate, but he has placed his family first. It still hurts.'

In another situation, the couple had to leave their home, Ireland, in order to be together. He came from a militant Catholic background and she from an equally belligerent Protestant family. Both fathers and all the brothers were in paramilitary organisations, actively fighting. Neither family could possibly conceive of one of their own marrying the hated 'enemy'. The young man in question had already had a battle to break free from the family tradition of violence. He simply wanted to pursue his profession of teacher in the hope, as he said, of bringing some sanity and peace into the situation by educating the young in a new way of being. She had felt the same. They met at an organisation that was trying to promote peace and reconciliation, and fell instantly and totally in love. Despite all family opposition, they married. It quickly became clear that his life was in danger from her family if they stayed in Ireland. They moved to England and cut off all contact with the families. Unfortunately, they also had to cut off from all their friends too, in case anyone inadvertently told their families. They simply did not know whom they could trust in that confused system of devout loyalties and religious bigotry.

When they looked at their soul purpose, it was to bring about harmony in a country in which both had incarnated on several occasions. One of these had been when 'the troubles' began. They had been parted by that, when one of them was killed, and vowed to be together again. They had also been married in much earlier times in the Ireland of the Dark Ages, paradoxically a time of much greater light in this now benighted country. It was an ecstatic marriage with a deep spiritual connection. But it was clear that, under prevailing conditions, they could not return to the Ireland of today and follow their souls' purpose. In order to be together, they simply had to leave their country and find a new life.

Written in the Stars?

Astrology provides a means of casting light on the dynamics of human relationships

—*Pauline Stone*[40]

We have already seen how contacts between people's astrological charts can indicate a basic similiarity and a sense of knowingness. When I told Mary, an astrologer friend of mine, that I was writing a book on soulmates, she immediately asked: 'Would you like my experience of my astrological soulmate?' The charts are shown below:

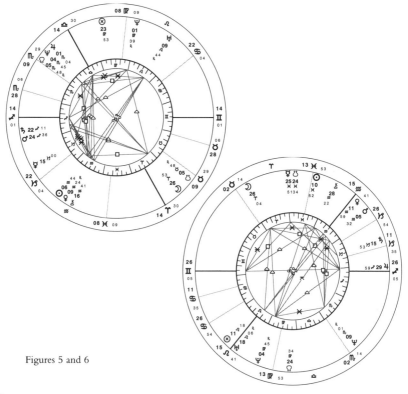

Figures 5 and 6

You do not need to be an astrologer to match the symbols around the outside of the charts (the zodiac signs) and see that six of the inner symbols (the planets) fall in the same signs. In both charts, the Moon and Venus, important relationship indicators because people feel so similar, are in Aries and Aquarius respectively – each highly independent signs. Venus in Aquarius is especially good at unconventional relationships and also friendship, and particularly those that are at a distance. When both Venuses fall in Aquarius, it can be a magnetic, electric attraction, but one without long-term commitment. In the relationship, Mary and Colin lived out their charts perfectly:

> Colin and I singled each other out. We both felt a strong karmic tie between us as soon as we met. We found many similarities of interest and ways of seeing things. We were also attracted to each other.
>
> As an astrologer, I calculated his chart and found all his planets and important points strongly aspecting [making a geometric relationship with] all my planets. This I had not seen before. We did feel so much in tune. We found it so easy to talk and be together.
>
> We wanted a relationship, but as we began to understand each other, we realised there was nothing there except knowing each other so well. We felt we had gone through so many karmic relationships and done everything already. There was nothing left to do together.
>
> We acknowledged it was good to see each other again and said our goodbyes. He lives on another continent now and has a separate life. We know the other is there and that is enough. I believe there are many kinds of soulmate – and know many past lives have been shared which determine what we will experience this time. We are all at different levels with different people significant to us – until we have worked through our karmic purpose. This was achieved with Colin and myself. We no longer need any relationship.

With so many planets in the same signs, and with Mary having a dreamy, romantically inclined Sun in Pisces, it would be easy for her to feel 'I've found perfect love, this person is so like me' – to have deluded herself that here was her one and only true soulmate. Fortunately her much more detached venusian energies were able to say: 'Hold on a minute, let's look at this.' Being an astrologer, she could recognise the pull to the past from the oh-so-comfortable Moon and Venus placed in the same sign, but she could also see that the indicators of their karmic purpose (the Moon's Nodes) were telling a different story. They were saying: 'Move away from the past and do your own thing. You have to go in very different directions to fulfil your karmic purpose. You are not destined to be together this time round.'

By the same post as I received Mary's contribution, Sue Boase's collection of stories also arrived. She had included an astrological soulmate tale also. One that shows how the movement of the planets can help to draw people to each other and propel them into their destiny together. The day-to-day movement of the planets around the sky, called transits, affects both our birthchart and our daily life. As we shall see, there are distinct cycles common to everyone at a certain age which are trigger points for change, and there are subtle interactions that are very personal to us and the unique chart for the moment we were born.

Belinda had married in her early twenties, but as she experienced her 'Saturn return' [when Saturn returns to the same place in the sky as it occupied when she was born, something which happens to everyone at about age twenty-eight or twenty-nine, signalling a time of reassessment] an inevitable divorce happened. She had one serious relationship during her mid-thirties, but when it ended with a broken heart, she resolved to give up men for life – which at the time seemed like a sensible decision since Pluto was moving through her scorpionic twelfth house [in other words, the deepest and most secret part of her chart was being activated by the most intense planet]. With Pluto, as any astrologer will tell you, it's 'Do or die'. This planet's transformatory qualities can cause intense distress unless the person is willing to let go with a capital L. Wise to this fact, she embarked on a series of intensive healing courses and started to work as an alternative therapist and counsellor – appropriately plutonian activities.

However, several years later as Pluto neared her Ascendant [the face we present to the world and a point at which we make things conscious], she began to feel huge shifts of energy inside which often took the form of depression followed by bouts of spiritual elation. She also felt that her heart was preparing to open, especially as Pluto, when it conjoined her Ascendant, would also make aspects to Venus and the Moon in her chart [that is, make a geometric relationship activating the energy of these planets]. While this was lining up, Uranus began moving into her own birthday sign of Aquarius, again aspecting her Venus and Moon. Now the universe can crack a few good jokes through the energy of Uranus but mix in the immense power and compulsion of Pluto and that is something else entirely. [It's like a quark meeting anti-matter. That Pluto-Venus contact can activate the 'emotional black hole' syndrome, the antithesis of the uranian free spirit.] Belinda watched what was manifesting around her with great interest, grateful that she was at least aware of the karmic implications of astrological energies – but nothing could prepare her for what was to come [Uranus is after all the planet of unpredictable change].

As the planetary energies began to assert themselves, she began to feel an overwhelming urge to completely change her life, draw in a partner and move home. So, accompanied by a fellow Aquarian friend, she spent a week visiting her favourite sacred places, where she ceremonially 'left her singleness behind'. She returned home feeling very much at peace with herself and excited about the future.

Two days later when her plans to play tennis were thwarted by poor weather, she decided on the spur of the moment to visit a friend who had recently moved to the area. The two immediately sat down to catch up on the gossip over a cup of tea. The door opened and in walked Jonathan, a young man who happened to be staying in the house for a short while. As he sat down across the room from Belinda, she witnessed an extraordinary occurence, which left her open-mouthed. She 'saw' a stream of energy from his heart meet a stream of energy from her heart in the centre of the room. These energies seemed to entwine around each other and then ascend together rapidly through the ceiling! [A highly uranian experience]. The young man also seemed to realise that something out of the ordinary was happening and in a short space of time had contrived to get Belinda alone by taking her to a local vegetarian takeaway for lunch supplies. As they walked towards his car, she looked up at him and said: 'Hello, I know you.' He replied: 'Thank you for recognising me.' With that, they joined hands.

On shutting the car door, he turned to her and said: 'I want to know all about you.' This seemed the most natural thing in the world for him to say; yet it seemed to them both that he already knew. On returning to the house laden with goodies, Belinda began to feel completely overpowered by the situation, so made her excuses to leave. A few hours later the phone rang. She knew it was him and with a mixture of dread and excitment picked up the receiver.

They met the following day where they learnt more about each other, including to her horror that he was fourteen-and-a-half years younger. Any feelings which were surfacing within her immediately met a stone wall. There was no way she was going to become emotionally involved with someone so much younger. Uranus had indeed thrown in the joker. He too felt very challenged by the age difference; yet they both knew they had something to do together. As the week progressed, they spent a lot of time trying to understand the plutonian intensity of their need to be with one another, each as baffled as the other. It was during the second week that Jonathan threw caution to the wind and suggested they move into a house together.

Against all reason, Belinda immediately agreed. To this day she says that she just knew that this is what they had to do, even though all her friends said she was insane. Jonathan promptly disappeared abroad for a few weeks, leaving Belinda to battle with her terror of the havoc this new future was going to wreak in her life. She spent much of her time drumming up every excuse in the world not to go through with it.

On Jonathan's return, things became very strained between them; yet it seemed the dye was cast and there was little they could do apart from follow their destiny. Within a month Belinda found their perfect home, a thatched cottage nestling in the foothills of the South Downs – and within eleven weeks of meeting, including a hectic Christmas and New Year, they had set up home together to begin the most extraordinary relationship of their lives.

It wasn't until a few weeks later when things had calmed down a little that Belinda looked into Jonathan's astrological configurations. While Pluto was doing its dance with her Venus and Moon, it was squaring his Venus [a difficult relationship creating great challenge and compulsion]. There were no half measures to be had in this relationship. Added to which, his natal Pluto, Uranus and Mercury were conjoining her own Moon – in

Virgo, which happened to be his sun-sign. There were also many other aspects indicating an extremely powerful, no-holds-barred, metamorphic experience staring them straight in the eye.

Typical of Pluto's influence, they have just completed one of the most traumatic yet vital and transformative years of their lives, and although they have ongoing plutonian power struggles to contend with, underlying that is a deep, honest and sincere love which has taken its time to mature. A couple of months ago they both knew it was make or break time, so they chose to go to a joint rebirthing session. Both were deeply affected by the experience, and rather than parting them, it pushed them deeper into their relationship. It helped them to sort out their constant power battles because both had witnessed the other in the depths of emotional trauma.

They have now learnt that there is no point in trying to control or manipulate their relationship, and both have come to accept and respect the part that Pluto plays in their lives. As for being soulmates? 'Well, that's one way of putting it,' says Belinda. 'If he is my soulmate, he couldn't be further from what I imagined. It's warts and all with us, and never a dull moment. Yet I love him far more completely than any other man I have been with and I have certainly learnt more about myself than I have with anyone else. We have both invested an enormous amount of time and energy into this relationship, and although it is difficult, we are now at the stage when we are really excited at the prospect of what is yet to come.'

More Than Just an Illusion?

The passion that left the ground to lose itself in the sky

—*Robert Browning*

One of the more extraordinary soulmate stores I have heard came from someone who had fought in the Vietnam War. He maintained that the drugs he took then, many of them unknowingly, had literally 'blown his mind' and that he now inhabited a different level of consciousness. As I discovered later, he had been diagnosed schizophrenic and hospitalised for some time. Everyone he had consulted so far had said he was suffering from delusions, that his experience was 'unreal', a psychotic fantasy. Now, he was in England trying to make sense of his experience. His story had an internal structure and consistency that made sense to me, no matter how others viewed it. It incorporated aspects that I had heard from many people, and even experienced myself. Was it all an illusion, were we all 'mad', or was he tuning into a univeral experience? Did he indeed have access to another level of consciousness and to glimpses of the future? (Certainly much of the seemingly more weird and way out beliefs he had have since come into mainstream thought, but as these are not a part of his soulmate experience we will not be looking at them here.)

He came to see me for several sessions, during which his story gradually unfolded. One of his first questions was whether I believed that we had a soulmate, and if so, could someone have a soulmate who was not in a physical body. I told him I did indeed believe in soulmates, but not necessarily in the conventional fashion. And that, yes, I did believe we could have a soul companion who was not incarnated but who remained very close to us.

He recounted to me that he had met his soulmate briefly and then she died. As this part was too confused and painful for him to relate coherently and he became agitated whilst talking about it, it was something I went back to much later. He wanted to do a regression to find out more about their previous contact – of which he had had several glimpses. I asked him to tell me more of his story first. Partly I felt I needed to check out his mental state before we looked at the possibility of regression (it is not something I would undertake with anyone in a psychotic state), but I also felt that he needed simply to be heard at this stage. Listening to someone's story in an accepting way can help to clarify exactly what is going on for them. I did not make a judgement as to how true it was or how much of a delusion he was under. Clearly this was his reality. If I could enter into it with him, then maybe we would both understand.

Eventually it emerged that when his soulmate died, she began to appear to him. At first in dreams, and then more and more often he would 'see' her around him. Then, he found himself out of his physical body and able to be with her. They inhabited a world that was, superficially, solid and 'real' but in which they could move around at will and in which thoughts and feelings were totally visible. To me it sounded exactly like the less physical realm to which we pass after death and into which we can venture from time to time when we leave our physical body behind. I had had enough experiences of this place myself, accompanied many people there, and read sufficient accounts, both ancient and modern, to accept this as a valid experience.

He said that, right from the start, they had sexual experiences together which were like nothing in the physical world. It was a total merging, a joining at the soul level. Again, this is supported by empirical evidence. Many accounts exist of such experiences. Eventually a soul marriage was performed. They took vows of eternal fidelity. He considered himself married. The only difference to ordinary, everyday marriage was that he had to leave his body to join his wife.

His wife had then communicated to him that they had a mission. They were to help those on earth understand about these other levels of being. To accept that death was not the end of existence. Soon, many people would find themselves in similar soul marriages. It was when he began to talk of this to his family and friends – and of the other somewhat more bizarre communications he was receiving – that he was hospitalised.

Now he wanted to know more. He, like so many 'schizophrenics', was convinced of the validity of his experience. Although the content of much of what he told me was bizarre and could be described as paranoid, it was nothing I had not heard before from other, supposedly 'sane' people. I suggested to him that he should write it all down in the form of a novel as the world might not be ready yet to read it as fact. He began this task, but was insistent that some of the answers at least would be found in the past.

I took him into regression to check out his previous connections with his 'wife'. In every one, he seemed to have met her and then one or other of them died before the relationship could develop. Eventually he vowed: 'Next time we will have a relationship no matter what.' I asked him to go right back to the beginning of their association. What he came up with was like something out of Plato and other, much earlier esoteric writings. A being, non-physical, and totally one was drifting blissfully through the cosmos. It was struck in half and the two pieces went hurtling off to opposite ends of the universe. Across aeons of time they searched for each other. When they met again, it was at a time of great cataclysm. Scarely had they met when they were parted again. This was the beginning of the cycle of meeting and parting, joining and losing, which seemed to spread over a great time span. It really did feel as though these were two parts of one soul weaving and entwining only to part again. He was quite convinced that she was literally his other half. Eventually, when they had done the work they had to do, he would leave earth and they would merge and become one again.

Clearly there are psychological and psychotherapeutic explanations that could be given here. We could look on his 'lost love' as representing his own inner feminine energies, the anima, from which he felt cut off. We could also see it as an externalisation of the enormous shock his psyche underwent in the trauma of Vietnam – the killing of all that was 'female': kindness, compassion, receptivity, sensitivity, caring, love. All qualities he had received from his soulmate in that brief contact before she was so brutally taken from him. We could see their 'marriage' as his way of reintegrating this lost part of himself. But something else could be going on here.

When we were finally able to talk about where he first met his love in his present life, he told me she had died in Vietnam. They had met and spent a little time together in the town near his base. Later, his platoon had been attacking a village, they opened fire and suddenly there she was. He had reached out to her as she reached out to him, but his buddy, convinced she was Vietcong and was trying to kill him, had shot her. She was ripped virtually in two by the bullets. He then had a complete breakdown, but in the madness that was Vietnam, no one seemed to notice. Taking refuge more and more in drugs, he eventually returned home to the States, a bombed-out wreck. But, at the same time, he was experiencing a rich life on another plane. He certainly felt his marriage was both valid and fulfilling. Who am I to say which was fantasy and which was reality. I'm with Shakespeare's Hamlet on this one:

> *'There are more things in heaven and earth, Horatio,*
> *than are dreamt of in (y)our philosophy.'*

Years earlier I had met a woman with a similar story. She was 'joined to' Thomas Chatterton, a fairly obscure eighteenth century poet who had poisoned himself at the age of seventeen. For the English Romantic poets of the nineteenth century he was the epitome of neglected genius. English graduates sometimes studied him, but few other people had heard of him until comparatively recently when his story was presented on British television. This woman's experience began long before this last event however.

According to her, they had been together across the centuries. He was her one and only soulmate, but he was not in incarnation now. He was manifesting through her from another level of being. Their experience of lovemaking was, however, at a physical level. Eventually she came to believe that he manifested in her physically as well. She developed breast cancer and was convinced that the lump was Chatterton making his appearance. This was not a woman who would have been immediately diagnosed as schizophrenic or suffering from delusions. Apart from this one somewhat unorthodox belief, she was the epitome of upright

English middle class suburbia. Unfortunately, I lost touch with her and have no idea of the outcome of her story. I do know, however, that she was longing to be reunited with her soulmate, so, presumably, she joined him in death.

In yet another experience, a woman met her soulmate every night in her dreams to make passionate love. Sexual magick is an ancient art and they had practised it before. She said it was a meeting on the astral plane. Both left their physical bodies behind and journeyed to this other place. In everyday life, he was married and she lived alone but they worked together. They never discussed their strange affair, but each knew how the other felt. She was convinced he was her soulmate and that somehow they would find a way to be together. Eventually, however, it became clear that he would not leave his wife. She broke off the affair but was desolated at the loss of her soulmate.

Many 'discarnate souls' make their appearance in regression work. They may be old soulmates, comrades in arms, chance acquaintances, children who were never born, or a myriad other connections – but they hover close. They are connected to our soul. Depending on how you look at it, the entity is loosely or tightly attached to the etheric or spiritual level of the person who is here on the earth. Some people see these entities as being rather like a psychic vampire who lives life through the incarnated person. Others see them as strongly influencing that person, or guiding them in some way. It is rather like the biblical concept of possession, although discarnate soulmate experiences are rather more benevolent. What is clear is that the discarnate soul is held and attracted to the person on earth. To understand how this can be, we need to go back to previous lives and those vows we make, such as 'Next time we will have a relationship no matter what' or 'I'll never leave you.' If we desire something strongly enough, or if we fail to free ourselves from our vows, we could well find ourselves in similar relationships.

The Mirror of our Being

We are mirrors of stellar light and we cast this light outward as...
magnetic attraction, characterizations, desires

—*W. B. Yeats*[41]

Our soulmate is the mirror of our being. If we lived alone, in isolation, would we ever come to know our self fully? This seems to be a task for our soulmate: bringing to us face to face with all the issues that need our attention, all our karmic lessons and ingrained patterns, all those unrecognised and unloved aspects of our self that we have been avoiding for so long; offering us the opportunity to love. And also bringing to us the love we seek. This love may not always be apparent at an everyday level of being; it may have become warped and twisted, but it is there at the level of the soul, at the place where we make our deepest connection. If we seek love conditionally, if we limit it, put 'ought's and buts' onto it, try to hedge it around with cast-iron guarantees, then what we get back will be conditional love. If we approach love with the view: 'If you are right, then I must be wrong', or 'You are doing this to me', then we will never resolve the duality of an I and You position. If we always see what we are seeking 'out there' in someone other, we can never be whole. But, if we seek love unconditionally, open to whatever is, then we will receive unconditional love.

We all have different needs and expectations around love. Let us go back to those explanations of how soulmates arose. In Plato, yes, there are two souls seeking to merge back into the wholeness they once knew. You might be one of those souls. In which case, you are desperately looking for your idyllic partner who accepts, loves, cherishes and understands, as no one else can. But say you are one of the satellites of the Hindu oversoul, expected to take all your experience back into the group, so that the whole can learn and grow. How will you then become whole unless you merge back into the oversoul from which you came? Can you find completeness in another soul? Is that what you are here for? Unlikely. And how about those of us who came out of the soul group of Western esotericism? Do we have to merge with each and every part of the soul group before we can find lasting love? Do we need to redefine our view of relationship, to open it up to a much wider meaning, including everyone with whom we interact? Should we perhaps be seeking completeness in our self, in our inner union, so that through our learning the greater self can expand? This is the experience of those who grow through their soulmate contacts.

I particularly wanted to include in this book an experience told by both partners and preferably by someone who had a psychotherapy background with the insights that would give. The couple I choose, Christie and Tyrell, had extremely interesting synastry between their astrological charts. They had the Neptune–South Node contact that so often feels like 'Here is my soulmate at last' and which can be oh so right, or oh so very deluded – and I knew they were finding it difficult to work their way through what was proving to be a problematic relationship, even though it had seemed so 'right' when it began. In their case, it was made more difficult through working in different countries and having to maintain very different lifestyles. Yet I was always aware of a very deep love between them. One of the reason's I asked for their story was that I felt the objectivity of looking at it from outside, of asking: 'How do I really perceive this relationship?' might help to throw new light on the relationship – in other words, for them to look into the mirror of their being.

When I had looked at their astrological connections two years previously, it had seemed to me that they truly were mirrors for each other. There was a very powerful sexual attraction, but also a sense of 'knowing each other from before'. However they approached life, and relationships, in totally different ways. Communication was important for Tyrell; for him closeness involved shared thoughts and feelings rather than sexual contact. For the much more tactile Christie, shared sensual and sexual experiences would lead to emotional closeness. Each had the astrological indicators of the problems the other was encountering. So, each had a huge difficulty with intimacy and a desire to run away from it all. Both had the expectation that they were unlovable, and what love they could get would be cold and distant, and in addition Christie had the 'Love hurts' scenario. Tyrell, on the other hand, had the ingrained expectation that he would not be heard: he had a deep communication wound. They shared a freedom–commitment dilemma, but Tyrell's Venus in particular wanted to be free. Christie played out this part of the relationship because she commuted between countries for her work, leaving Tyrell on his own for months at a time. So he felt abandoned where he would otherwise have felt trapped. She, on the other hand, felt trapped where she needed to be free.

Her Descendant (one of the relationship indicators) was in the same sign as his Sun – authoritarian Capricorn. He represented what she was expecting from relationships, and we see what we expect rather than what actually is. His Moon and Venus were in the sign that made up most of her seventh house – the relationship house. He had qualities she, knowingly or unknowingly, sought in a man. But it would be like a mirror image, and, as with most people in this position, it was doubtful if she would recognise him as that mirror or see herself in it. Due to the astrological configurations, he, on the other hand, had more opportunity to recognise: 'This is me, that is you.' But it would be difficult. Anything that activated her Venus (the love planet) pressed her 'I can't be loved' button. Anything that activated his Venus pressed his 'I want to be free' urge. He perceived her as taking her freedom, while she experienced him as cold and unloving. The placement of the Nodes suggested that she was trying to move out of losing herself in relationships to find her independence; he was seeking to merge, to find union with a partner – but each saw that in the other.

In the first draft I received from Christie, I got the 'There isn't any love there' saga. The second draft was cut in half by the fax machine (interesting and most symbolic I felt!). The third had the last page missing. Finally the full story arrived with its acknowledgement of the love they share. But, as she said later: 'This has kept me locked in a battle which had nothing to do with the relationship. It has kept me from recognising the love that is there. And yet, because I recognise the projection of the coldness and lack of love, how can I be sure the love I perceive isn't also a projection?' – a difficult dilemma indeed.

The perils of a handsome French stranger

A memory or feeling of love lost has haunted me since my first sweetheart at fifteen, with whom I had my first child. I used to cry and not understand what the tears were about. Writing this story makes my heart both ache and pound with anxiety.

This story represents a shard of my soul… a piece of the stream of consciousness which inhibits my ability to experience ordinary human affection and love on an ongoing basis.

Each man I've been with this life has reflected a bittersweet sorrow along with the deep love I yearn to share with a partner. I have always had a man around to share my life with and, with only one exception, have fond memories of each one. Somewhere inside me there's been a caution… a feeling that the person is not the right man for me. That transparent layer of indecision affected my self-esteem and peace.

This all changed twelve years ago when I realised how this sense of caution was diluting the quality of relationship I had with my then partner. I allowed myself the privilege of loving one man deeply and fully and our spiritual connection is very strong today even though our physical relationship ended in 1990. He and I used to talk about things concerning the soul, Aquarian things. He challenged me to communicate love from the ache in the heart, and we taught one another volumes about our humanity. I was once told if I would stick with the relationship until spirit moved to end it, my diamond inside would be polished.

I went to Egypt in April of 1990 and the first night encountered a male spirit who came to me in a vision and took me to a beautiful chamber where we were both wearing long, flowing white gowns. I was overjoyed to see him and remember a warm feeling inside filling me with anticipation. Then my mother opened a door and came into the room. I pulled back and withdrew my affection towards the man, at which point my mother smiled and gave me permission to be with him. After she left the room and closed the door behind her, he picked me up and laid me back on a chaise longue couch. I thought we would make love, but instead he told me it was not time, kissed me gently on the forehead and disappeared.

I was in Egypt a month and barely slept for the joy I felt in having met him once again. During a later ceremony at Sakkara I knew that I would sell my home of eighteen years upon my return from the journey, the six-year relationship would end by Christmas (no signs at that point), and I had to give up over-mothering my daughter. All three things happened and I set out on a new course in life. I chose not to date, knowing I would remember the feeling of the man when I met him. I immersed myself in my work and began to write in 1991.

In December of 1993 I had a dream that the man from Egypt was coming into my life. I usually wore a ring on my left hand wedding finger to deter suitors in general and in the dream I took the ring off. The next morning I physically took the ring off and tucked it away. I felt the same deep joy and clarity I had felt in Egypt. Friends started asking me if I had met someone and fallen in love. I just smiled to myself in anticipation.

A couple of months passed and in early February of 1994 I was warned by an intuitive that I would meet a man and want to run away, but not to – because this would be an important relationship. I said I knew my partner was coming and left it at that.

The next morning, a lazy Monday, I met Tyrell, a man with whom I immediately felt a strong attraction. He rang me that night and we had tea Tuesday at 11am. I soon noticed a clear, thick wall between us causing us to have a difficult time communicating.

On Wednesday I received a two-page 'sorry I'm not interested' letter – 'You're a Leo and I've done that!' I wrote him back that day. Thursday I rang him at work to say I respected his opinion; yet I thought there might be value in our getting to know one another. Although he was polite, he was steadfast that he wasn't interested, and I hung up the phone with tears running down my cheeks. This was odd given the brief time we'd spent together! Also I wasn't that keen on anything getting in the way of my work. I went away for the weekend and walked along the country roads trying to make sense of the brief encounter and the deep feelings stirring in me.

He called me Monday afternoon and asked if I wanted to go out for a meal.

I said yes. We were comfortable together and got on well. He called me the next evening and asked me if I believed in monogamy. I said I believe in being true to myself and that includes being loyal in partnership. We spent that weekend together. We laughed, lay belly to belly snuggling for hours, hugged continuously. Seven months later we had a private wedding ceremony with no family or relations – his choice of marriage, which began our nightmare. The communication broke down completely and I felt he wanted me to go.

Life with Tyrell was chaotic and exhausting. He's a psychotherapist and was constantly on about how I was 'projecting on him'. I'm not a therapist and found being a patient rather than lover and wife quite a shock. He enjoys words and presents to express love and I enjoy physical touching to express my deep feelings. It was obvious that neither of us had our needs met. I said I would go, which made him feel insecure. What a waste of energy.

I went away on business early each day and when I returned he was distant, not wearing his wedding ring, and constantly telling me how much I'd hurt him. I wanted to leave and get on with my life. Instead I stayed with him to see what I could learn. I had recurrent bladder infections and was unable to reach orgasm. A few months later I saw a Chinese medicine doctor-homeopath who prescribed essences and promised I would be able to orgasm in no time at all. He also detected a layer of depression. I took the remedies and I was finally able to relax and reach orgasm... Ah relief! Some months later my bladder symptoms cleared also.

Tyrell had been with his soulmate, his wife of twelve years, and they had parted years before we met. Later, after rethinking his concept of soulmate, he felt his sister was the closest thing he had to a soulmate. This didn't surprise me because they were very close. I told him I thought our family dog Max was my soulmate! I wondered if either of us was even remotely available for this exercise in love.

I remembered a past life clearly in which my partner was a French trader and I was a native American woman. I called Tyrell 'Pierre', which he didn't like being British, so I stopped. I always also had a strong sense that there was a spell to keep us apart. He dismissed my memories since he had no sense of them himself and said I was projecting.

The strange energies continued between us, and Tyrell mentioned his distress to his therapy supervisor, who recommended a 'magician' who would straighten out my 'unhealthy projections'. When we finally got to see him, the first words he said were: 'There's no love here.' He then proceeded to describe the Indian life I remembered and confirmed there was a spell designed to keep us apart for ever. I trembled and wept as the memories swamped my senses. Pierre had asked me to leave my people and go with him. I loved him and agreed. My people refused to let me go. I thought about what they said and one night crept out to tell him I would not go with him. When I got to him, he was having sex with another woman. I was heartbroken. Within seconds a spell-laced arrow pierced his heart and he lay dead before me. There was a second arrow which would have taken my life. Instead I was left with the sight of the man I loved betraying me in a way which I had not imagined. It was not the way of my people. Heartbroken, I was taken back to my people, married the man I had been promised to before the French man came, and had several children.

During the session, I remember looking across the room at Tyrell, who kept saying as if to expose me, 'See, she is projecting! She does this all the time! She's the problem.' There was no mutuality in the memory or any compassion from my husband for the grief I was experiencing – nothing to remember together.

The magician stopped time and pointed to my husband's dialogue, and warned me that staying in the relationship could be hazardous to my spiritual health. Remember, this is the therapist Tyrell 'forced' me (my victim/authority issue) to see because he thought I was projecting something which had nothing to do with him. On his side, it was to sort out the shadow, so we could find out what was happening with the energies. Coincidentally, he did go along to see the magician later and had the spell removed – just in case – but he has no memory of the experience and still believes I am projecting something that has nothing to do with him. The magician warned me that once the spell was removed there might be no connection left between this man and me. What a relief after all the heartache.

Within a couple of weeks we went to see a European doctor who looks at blood cells and diagnoses what the cells in the body are up to. After meeting with my husband, the doctor said my husband did not trust me, and when there is no trust, there is no love. This confirmed what the magician said. I left the office saddened and determined to clear this matter up. To me that means taking responsibility for identifying the emptiness in my heart in the light of day. It has been a difficult year to integrate the depths of consequences following from the chaos of the infatuation I felt for the Frenchman. The spell was meant to scatter the energies and keep us apart for ever.

That was a year ago and I have learned much since that time. I am grateful for the confirmation from the magician. Grateful for the deep healing and release, and the connection I feel with all people has deepened.

I travelled to the Yucatan this past February on my own, keenly aware that there is no longer a man 'out there' for me. I have stayed with myself and the sweetness of the heartfelt memories intact before this man (the Frenchman) crossed my path so long ago.

The greatest gifts of this marriage are that I have got my heart back from the Frenchman, released the energies of the spell, and have freedom to begin again. I was also able to grieve deeply for the sense of loss from 'giving my heart' to a French stranger in another time. I identified the emptiness of living without welcome, the darkness of losing the love and acceptance of a community for a stranger.

According to a recent meeting with an astrologer, our charts are such that we are opposed in every way – leaving us to 'agree to disagree' and struggle to meet in the middle on most issues. This information was tremendously liberating.

Tyrell and I don't laugh. We don't sleep well together. We barely touch one another. We are strangers once again. This reflects our communication breakdown. We are both looking deeply within ourselves for clues to continuing to spend time learning from one another. But living without the tenderness and affection of the remembered love with a group of people haunts me. I ache because I do remember. This is the journey of my soul and I will continue to follow my yearning.

Tyrell has offered a good lesson for my heart, one which I'm still learning. I do love him and somehow always have.

We can see just how different Christie's approach to life is and glimpse some of the difficulties she and Tyrell encountered in entering into each other's reality when we read her husband's account of the same relationship:

Perseus meets the Medusa:
Tyrell's story

I was once married to someone I perceived as my 'soulmate'. We had much in common and an intuitive knowing of each other. After twelve years the marriage ended, causing me to examine many things, including what a soulmate was. My resulting belief was that there was no such thing: if we had all evolved from an original point of being, then we were all equally connected to each other and therefore equally capable of loving and being loved by anyone. It was simply down to choosing whom we wanted to be with. I filed the concept of soulmates under 'romantic notions' until I had further evidence.

Over the following years my sister, Sara, and I spent more time together than we ever had done. We shared the joys and pains we were experiencing as we moved in and out of relationships, and noticed that we were constantly being faced by the same learning challenges. We would have similar 'ahas!' of realisation at the same time, similar thoughts, similar relationships. We also noticed that the degree to which we were able to support each other, and feel supported, far exceeded that of any other relationship we had. There was something 'twin-like' happening, as though we were taking our learnings back to a shared point of being. There was a sense of working for the same goal through parallel experiences. Even now, we both stand bewildered in our separate relationships, confused as to 'what the right thing is', awaiting the mutual 'aha!'

One evening we played around with the 'what if' of our being some sort of soulmates. The next day, Sara came across the writings she had made a few years before at a 'write-in', where hours are spent in endless writing without any purpose other than to clear creative blocks to the unconscious. Sara had never bothered to read what she had written until that day. Among the many things that she had absolutely no recall of writing was the sentence: 'Your brother is your soulmate.' This provided a comforting thought that there may be a special relationship in the world, helping with the feelings of existential aloneness, but not a belief that it was so.

My first words on meeting Christie were, 'I know you!' And somehow, I did. I was immediately attracted to her but inside, part of me was shouting 'Keep away!' There was something in her that was too challenging. Having 'suffered' in the den of a Leo a year before, I was unwilling to be drawn in by the kitten aspect and initially resisted, yet here was something totally dissimilar to any previous relationship: I saw Christie as a woman, not as a girl.

The differences between us were many. I was quiet, reflective and fairly solitary [Capricorn Sun and Aquarius Moon]. Christie was loud, expressive and very sociable [Leo Sun and Moon]. We were from different countries and cultures. And though I believed differences were important for a relationship to be 'active' and growth promoting, there seemed to be too much to deal with, with her. I not only saw the beauty of who she was, but also saw the shadow in her that she was not owning. In previous relationships I had considered it was part of the process to draw this part out but somehow knew it would not be easy with Christie. I didn't realise at that time how distorted that belief was!

Christie, however, gently pushed to get to know each other better – and I agreed. Seven months later, we were married. The seven months had been an intense and romantic time, much of it spent apart in our respective countries communicating through long letters and phone calls. Our commitment to each other was total and surprising. Neither of us believed we would ever marry again.

We chose the date and time of the ceremony astrologically in order to face as much of ourselves as we could within the relationship. I'm not sure that with hindsight we would make the same choice…

The conflicts began immediately – and we were both shocked. For my part, I couldn't believe this was the person I had fallen in love with. Where she had initially seemed the woman I would most like to be with if I were a woman, she was quickly becoming the opposite. I was training as a psychotherapist at the time, but my skills of objectivity were swept aside in the onslaught of feelings.

I was well aware of the stages of relationship and did not expect the romantic phase to last for ever, but I felt overwhelmed by the power of what was happening. All I could do was hold onto the belief, 'There must be a reason'.

The inability to communicate was the biggest factor. I had always put communication at the top of my list of 'absolute necessities' in a relationship. Suddenly I found myself unable to make any impression on Christie with my thoughts and feelings. It was as though I didn't exist. All my issues of not being seen or heard flooded forward. Frustration grew. She expressed similar feelings. I felt steam-rollered, manipulated, misunderstood, misquoted, mistreated and powerless in the relationship. I reached a point where I actually believed there was something seriously wrong with my perception of Christie… and the world, to be in such a chaotic state. My reality was being thrown up for examination [reflecting my Moon sign, Aquarius and much else besides].

The knowledge that I loved this person was consistently present. The other consistency was the sense of being in a relationship, yet very alone.

I slowly began to come to terms with the fact that I was 'out of control'. Everything I saw Christie 'doing to me' I had done in previous relationships. Everything negative I had felt about myself, I now felt in a magnified form. Here was the perfect mirror for me to gaze at. Here was 'instant karma'. Whether Christie really was 'doing it to me' began to dwindle in significance. The importance was in how I dealt with it. Do I really want to feel hurt, rejected, angry? Or can I move into that more adult place of acceptance? And do I want to even bother?

One day I requested guidance and selected a book at random from the bookshelves. Equally at random I selected a page. It was the myth of Perseus. In the flush of manhood he accepts the king's challenge to go and cut off the head of Medusa. Any man who looked upon the horrendous face of Medusa, framed by writhing snakes, became paralysed with shock. Medusa is the image for the 'negative feminine' – the dark shadow aspect. Perseus took with him a burnished shield – not to protect himself in the usual way, but to use as a mirror, so that he did not look at Medusa directly but through the reflection instead. He manages to slay Medusa and from her head flies Pegasus, potent with the positive feminine qualities of creativity and spirituality. Perseus then went on to free Andromeda from being sacrificed – another metaphor for the freeing of the anima, the feminine aspect. This was the perfect summary of what was happening. In the past I would encourage the Medusa to come forward in relationships and my male part would become transfixed by her darkness. I would use the 'niceness' of my feminine to try to change her – and, of course, it didn't work. I would be constantly disappointed by my partner and never feel potently male. All of this I also experienced as a child in relationship to my parents.

With Christie, everything seemed exaggerated. I would often say to her that I was 'shocked', 'horrified' and 'appalled' by things she did or said, and I don't use these words lightly. My whole being would experience absolute horror. I was still trying to deal with the dark feminine by 'looking to her' and becoming transfixed. When Perseus held up his shield as a mirror, he was looking at his own dark feminine instead of someone else's. But without Medusa's existence he would never have had cause to look in the mirror.

The sword that Perseus used to slay Medusa was given to him by Hermes, the 'crosser of boundaries' who is connected to moving between the conscious and unconscious. It was clear that the challenge was to face, and accept, my own unconscious aspects of the dark feminine in order to free the positive. Presumably Medusa's death results then from natural causes!

I feel this is where I am now, working to slay my horror of Medusa by 'allowing' the feminine in all her forms to come through, and learning how to use my masculine to hold the form of my life for it all to happen. At the same time, all this affects my relationship with Christie through a progressive acceptance of her.

For as long as I can remember, my interpretation of the word 'love' has been 'complete and unconditional acceptance'. When I react to my partner, I am not accepting, and the only path to acceptance of something in others is to first find it in ourselves and accept that.

Anyone who helps us on that road of self-investigation and self-acceptance has to be a messenger from God. Yet that messenger can only ever be perceived as someone to run as far away from as possible – or be destroyed, which is surely why 'soulmates' is not a term usually applied to such relationships. We like comfort, not confrontation!

Would I prefer a warm, cosy, supportive relationship? Yes, and yes again, but it's a bit like the mountain that has to be climbed because it's there – I just hope there's a good view from the top.

Whether my own story will transpire as beautifully as Perseus' is yet to be seen. By its nature, mythology describes the ideal rather than the norm and it may be that I am not a 'hero'.

I still don't believe in soulmates, but I do believe that the gift Christie has given me, forcing me to look deep inside, is every bit as valuable as that of the more conventionally accepted version of 'mutuality'. And who knows, perhaps one day we may have that too – if we manage to stay together...

Despite their apparent differences, these are two people who still seem so right together. Despite the cultural differences, they are so alike in many ways that they could almost be twins. When my daughter met Tyrell she said: 'I just knew he had to be Christie's husband. He couldn't be with anyone else. They are so alike.' Perhaps now that Christie has recovered her heart from that handsome French stranger she will be able to make her own inner marriage with the 'Egyptian' who is waiting. With Tyrell having faced his own dark feminine, the relationship will inevitably change – hopefully for the better.

Did You Give Your Heart Away?

What of soul was left, I wonder, when the kissing had to stop?

—Robert Browning

Right from the start, I gave you my heart...
I gave you my heart but you wanted my soul...
That kiss you stole held my heart and soul...

As these lines from popular songs show, we live in a culture that equates love with giving away our heart – and our soul, handing over a part of ourselves into someone else's keeping. In adolescence, and later life too, we carelessly give away our heart and, when we part, we forget to take it back. It is not only the twentieth century that has seen things this way. Shakespeare speaks of '[bearing me to] her, where I my heart, safe-left, shall meet'. Ancient Egyptian papyruses speak of the 'Lord of my heart'. The heart has always been equated with love. We talk of a broken-hearted lover, of giving our heart into safe keeping. How often when a lover leaves, or we leave, do we think to say: 'Excuse me, but can I have my heart back before we part, and, oh, by the way, I release us both from all those declarations of eternal love that we made?'

If we extend this tendency to hand over our heart back into other lives, how many parts of ourselves have we left behind? And who now holds them? Exercises to recover our hearts often produce surprises. As we change roles, interact in different ways, these 'keepers of our heart' may become our friend, our enemy, our parent, our child even. No wonder the soulmate boundaries blur. To free ourselves to find true love again, we may need to recover these fragments of our heart. To go back into the past and reclaim them.

Just how complex this can be, how many layers can be involved, is shown by Anita's experience:

I had been working for sometime on freeing myself from the control of a very powerful man who ran the company for which I worked. I considered him as a friend, and originally had been very attracted to

156

him. Indeed, for a couple of years I believed myself in love with him. I secretly harboured romantic visions of his becoming my lover or even my husband.

Through doing past-life work, I soon learned that this attraction did not belong to this lifetime, but was a residue from a past life in which we had been lovers, after which he had rejected me. I had remained unmarried and had died in traumatic circumstances. In that life, he had no longer wanted me as a lover, but had become very jealous if ever I had associations with other men, and had beaten me in his jealous rage. In my present lifetime, from the time I met him, I had found it impossible to start a relationship. I would meet men I was attracted to, but nothing would ever get off the ground. I feel now that he had somehow in that other lifetime drawn a veil over my emotions so that I could not see anyone else and that this carried over into our present contact.

Eventually, I knew I had to pluck up the courage to tell him about the past life, to express the feelings I had for him then, and to clear it for myself. I was very scared but managed to tell him. After a week or so, the infatuation I felt for him began to fade, and I felt sure I was free of him and ready to find a partner.

However, I found that the situation was still blocked. I tried working with it in as many ways as I could think of, but still couldn't resolve it. Then Judy suggested I should 'take back my heart'. A friend led me through the meditation. I saw the man, and could sense both aspects of him – past and present. He was carrying my heart in a box. I asked why he wanted to keep it and he said 'power'. I asked for higher help, and he eventually handed the heart over, and began to shrink and disappear. I then sent love to him, while keeping my heart. He said: 'Be happy. Bless you.' Before coming out of the meditation, I asked if there was anything else I needed to do. I saw the man saying in mock irritation: 'Clear off! You've finished!' I felt wonderfully free and clear of the situation.

Nevertheless, the relationship situation was still blocked for me. A few months later, I went into another regression to the previous lifetime. I found myself again talking to the man in question. The therapist said: 'What has he got that's yours?' and told me to go through his pockets. When I did, I found a ring. I took it back, and returned another one to him. Then I saw what had happened. We had exchanged rings to hold us together for ever. I saw the scene the day it happened, back in the eighteenth century. I was very young, and we were in the garden together, very flirty, but with a sinister undertone. I said: 'I give you my heart for ever'. He said: 'Ah, but I want your soul!' To my horror, I saw myself saying to him, 'I give you my soul' and we exchanged the rings. To me it was just playfulness and an expression of love, but to him it was deadly serious – he wanted total control of me. I had innocently allowed him to do this. So now I reframed the scene and saw myself saying to him: 'I give you my heart for as long as it is appropriate.' He asked: 'Will you give me your soul?' I replied: 'No! I will never give you my soul' and faced him with arms crossed. He nodded to me, acknowledging my power. It felt as if he had met his match.

I wanted to share this story as I was amazed at how many levels there can be to be released. If you think you've cleared something, but an area of your life still isn't working, then have another look. It was also interesting that this problem with relationships was not triggered until I met the man again in this lifetime. It was as though the veil came back and I could not see anyone else. However, once I let go of my view of him as a prospective lover, I was able to feel unconditional love for him. This was very different to how I felt when he still had the hold over me. Now I know I have reclaimed both my heart and soul.

False gurus

Tis an awkward thing to play with souls
And matter enough to save one's own

—Elisabeth Barrett Browning

A particularly insidious 'giving of the heart' arises in 'guru-worship'. The problem results from guru, teacher or mentor type figures who, consciously or otherwise, use their spiritual, intellectual or sexual power to bind their pupils or followers to them. These powerful figures may deliberately encourage total dependence as a way of gaining control. They have also been known to demand sexual favours to ensure promotion in the secular world, or to intimate that allowing the guru sexual favours will hasten spiritual enlightenment as part of an 'initiation' into the spiritual world – a passing on of energy. Even if a guru is not abusing his power, spiritual love between guru and pupil is often seen as an essential precursor to unification with 'the Beloved', i.e. God in whatever guise He, or She, is cast.

If we look at the life of the Sufi mystic Mevlana Celaleddin Rumi, we can see how the divine heart-fire is ignited between himself and his teacher, Shemseddin Tebrizi (the prose is somewhat quaint but beautifully conveys the feelings, so I have left it as it stands):

> *He [Mevlana] was returning home from the Medrese, in the middle of the street two hands suddenly grasped the reins of the mule he was riding on. The man was a wandering dervish and Mevlana not knowing who he was replied the questions of the Dervish without any ornamentation, sophistication and complexity. This straightforward and single-hearted answers got the Dervish excited and spurred stimulation in his soul. Getting off his mule Mevlana embraced the Dervish and they went home together. After that day the door of the soul of Mevlana was opened with the key of divine love.*

> *—Guidebook to the Shrine of Rumi, Konya*

This is a dramatic meeting with a traumatic relationship to follow. The dervish, Shems, disappears. Mevlana is devastated. Shems reappears. Mevlana is ecstatic. Jealous of his influence, Rumi's followers have Shems murdered:

> *Mevlana's lonesome bruised heart and confused mind never calmed then.. The absence of Shems influenced Mevlana deeply and was burnt by a flame of melancholy and trance, so that he was dragged into love's spell in an everlasting mystery.*

As Talat Sait, A Turkish commentator on the Dervishes pointed out:

> *This sequence of events was a perfect mystic phenomenon. For Mevlana, Shems constituted the embodiment of God as well as the symbol of humanity... in Shems' absence Mevlana was to undertake an arduous mystical search... [when Shems returned] Mevlana had found God again, this time to merge his soul utterly and inseparably.* [42]

The Western Sufi teacher Irina Tweedie's Indian guru employed powerfully abusive methods to break her will, but she still describes him in terms of a beloved.[43] Just to be allowed near him for a few moments, she would sit for hours in the baking sun without food or water as he had ordered. He had called to her over thousands of miles to be his disciple and she believed he had the right to total command over her life. Although she describes him in terms of a kindly, loving soul, his actions were harsh. As he was dying, it was her he chose to sit with him, until his mood altered and he sent her away again: an action which broke her heart. After he died, he was with her continuously. There is little difference in her account of him as guru and other people's account of life with a soulmate. The only divergence is that other people often look for a perfect, divine being who is a soulmate, whereas she believed she was meeting the divine in him.

It is not only overt gurus who use these methods. One charismatic leader of a New Age centre, whom we will call Arthur, greeted his guests (male and female) by psychically probing their lower chakras. Whether this was conscious or not, I do not know. But many, many people commented on it to me and I experienced it myself. It was extremely intimate, and intrusive. But other people found it sexually exciting and thought it was reserved especially for them. Almost everyone (male and female) who met Arthur thought 'he fancies me'. The result was a plethora of middle-aged women waiting to fall at his feet – or into his bed – and not a few men prepared to do the same. All were convinced this was their soulmate.

Unfortunately Arthur also had young people around, male and female, who all came under his spell. They were inducted into his own particular view of spirituality. He bound them so closely to him that they were unable to think for themselves. Each thought they were in a special relationship with him. Each had handed over their heart. No matter how badly he abused them, they looked on him as 'the most marvellous teacher'. He was extremely abusive, ranting and raving at them at the slightest provocation. He behaved like some of the Eastern gurus who feel that humiliation is the first essential in discarding the ego to become enlightened.

And then, suddenly they would be out. He would tell them they were too dependent, they needed to stand on their own feet. He behaved in exactly the same way in his sexual relationships, suddenly pulling out. Unfortunately, in no case did he give back the heart that had been so freely given. The young people and his ex-relationships were left in limbo. Tie cutting could help them, but it was taking back their heart that was the key to their ability to make a new life.

Reclaiming your heart

I find guided visualisation a useful tool in freeing from the past. It can be used to reframe incidents, to change the script, to put in the provisos that will make it 'as long as appropriate'. It can also be used to take positive action, such as reclaiming the heart. Visualisation is a powerful means of programming our subconscious energies. It is done in a relaxed state, which creates an 'altered state of consciousness'. The exercise can be memorised, taped or read aloud by a facilitator, perhaps with appropriate background music, allowing sufficient time for each stage. The advantage of having someone else work with you is that they can adapt to your timing and rhythm and you don't have to worry about forgetting a step.

Whilst some people see extremely clear pictures, others find them hazy, and some never really see anything in a visualisation. Looking up to the point slightly above and between your eyebrows helps images to form. If you are a non-visual person, try 'acting as if'. Let yourself *feel* each stage of the process. Indeed, you can act it out, moving around a room to create the right feel and having 'props' where appropriate.

You will need a comfortable place where you will not be disturbed for half an hour or so. You may like to sit in an armchair, or to lie on a bed. Remove any external distractions and create a quiet, peaceful atmosphere. Flowers or perfumed oils can help to create the right ambience.

You can do the following exercise with someone with whom you know you have had a close connection in your present life, or you can ask to be shown connections from other lives as well. It may not be necessary to know details of who they are, just to recognise that they do hold your heart. On the other hand, you may need to listen to their story and renegotiate any old promises made.

Exercise: Reclaiming your heart

Settle yourself comfortably and establish a gentle rhythm with your breath. Do not force it. Focus on your breathing for a few moments. As you breathe in, breathe in a sense of peace. As you breathe out, let go any tension you may be feeling. Each breath will take you deeper and deeper into relaxation. Soon your body will be feeling pleasantly relaxed, a deliciously warm, peaceful feeling will spread from the top of your head down to your toes. Give a big sigh of peaceful contentment.

[3 minutes]

Now focus your attention on your heart. Feel its beat, hear its sounds. As you listen to the rhythm of your heart and feel its pulsating beat, let yourself relax a little deeper. Slowly, let your heart transport you into another time and space.

[3 minutes]

You will find yourself standing in the temple of your inner heart. Its colour and dimensions are unique to you. Explore this temple; notice if it is broken anywhere. Notice if you meet anyone else (if so, remember to work with them in a moment). Recognise if there are heart strings pulling you in a certain direction. If there are, use a pair of golden scissors to cut the connection and then heal and seal this place with golden light.

[5 minutes]

You may already have become aware of someone who holds your heart, if so picture that person standing before you. If you have not yet recognised who holds your heart, ask to be shown this right now. (If there is more than one person, work on one at a time.)

[2 minutes]

You will see that this person holds a portion of your heart. It may appear symbolically. If so, look at its colour, shape and form. You may find that it is freely offered back to you, or you may find that the person wants to hold onto it. If they do, ask their reason. They may well feel that they have to look after you, or you may have made them a promise, or you may have given your heart into their keeping. If necessary thank them, release them, release yourself, whatever is appropriate. You will need to state firmly that it is now time to reclaim your heart.

[5 minutes]

Now, take a deep breath and focus all your attention. Very firmly and clearly, reach out and take this heart back. Welcome it back with love and place it once more within you.

[3 minutes]

(If you experience any problems, ask for a guide, a helper, your higher self or an angelic being to come to your aid. Having a firm intention is the best help you can have though.)

Repeat this reclaiming until there is no one left who holds a part of your heart. Check that you yourself do not inadvertently hold a piece of someone else's heart. If you do, surrender it willingly and allow it to return where it belongs. Then check the inner temple of your heart once again. You will probably find that it is looking much better. You may well find that the symbolic pieces of your heart decorate the walls. If it needs any further repair, use golden light.

[2 minutes]

Now consciously step out of that inner temple, but know that it is within your own heart, which is now whole and healed. Become aware of your breathing once again, and the beat of your heart. Slowly bring your attention back into the room. Take your attention down to your feet and ground yourself firmly. Picture a bubble of light enclosing you, sealing your energies, so that you are safe and protected. When you are ready, open your eyes. After a few moments reflection, get up and move around the room.

For ever and ever, amen?

Too long a sacrifice can make a stone of the heart.

—*W.B. Yeats*

We have already looked at several of the vows that can bind us to another soul: 'Of course I'll always be with you', 'I'll never leave you', 'I will always love you', 'You are the only one for me', 'To have and to hold from this day forth', 'We're going to be together next time round' are just a few of the promises we make. These promises trap both parties to the vow. In many marriages, the pair stayed together because there was no option, but with the heart, in the words of Yeats, turned to stone, and love, if it existed at all, turned to hatred or indifference. The couple were locked into that 'for ever and ever, amen' scenario. However, a pair of souls can become trapped by a vow that only one person makes, or even by the wishful thinking of one of the parties. You may find yourself part of a vow that says: 'I'll make him (or her) know what it is to suffer', or 'I could make him so happy if only...' You may also have demanded of someone else: 'Be there for me', for example. If so, you need to release them.

Occasionally an 'if only life' will surface in past-life regression. It is characterised by a certain quality of yearning, a wistful sense of 'this is how it should be' rather than a gutsy, full-blown reliving. I have come to see these 'relivings' as the fantasy that was being played out in someone's mind at the time rather than an actual event. So, if a spinster had romantic dreams of her future husband and these were never realised, they can well become imprinted as 'memory'. It was something I had already spotted when talking to elderly women about the First World War. So many of them nostalgically referred to 'my fiancé who was killed in the war, you know'. Of course, many men were killed then, but talking to other family members would often reveal that, far from an engagement, it had been a passing fling, or someone who had been admired from afar, or even the boy who lived down the road.

Equally, if someone is in a 'bad marriage', they will often look back wistfully to another suitor, 'If only I'd married him (or her)', they will say longingly, 'It would all have been different.' I'm not so sure it would: we tend to attract the same patterns to us. But this is not the point. It is the desire that imprints, the wishful thought, and, with the passing of time, it can be seen as fact. So, when I take someone back to look at the source of a soulmate contact, I bear in mind that it could have originated in the imagination. It might possibly be one-sided. Then again, it might not.

Exercise: To renegotiate a vow
(Follow the relaxation steps in the first exercise for the first few minutes)

Now picture yourself back at a point in time when you made a vow or a promise. (If you are unaware of when this was, ask to be shown.) Re-run the scene as it happened, but do not become too involved in it. Look on, do not take part. Notice who is present and what you are saying. If it is someone you do not recognise, ask who that person is in your present life.

[5-10 minutes]

Now look carefully at that vow. Is it still appropriate? Is it something you want to continue? Does it need to be reworded, or rescinded? Is it something from a past life that has inadvertently been carried over into the present? Have you demanded a vow from someone else that is holding them to you? If appropriate, ask for an advisor to come to discuss the matter with you. If it is a promise made to a soulmate, have them be with you outside the scene to join in the discussion. Check whether it needs to continue. Check also whether you made a promise to a soulmate between lives.

[5 minutes]

Then see yourself in that scene using the new wording. Be firm and clear: 'It is for this life only.' Or state clearly, 'I cannot do that' if what you are being asked will fetter your soul unreasonably. If the promise has to carry over into the present life, or if it has been made for or in the present life, set out the conditions under which it can operate. Make it clear that if your soulmate does not stick to the agreement, or if circumstances change, then the promise will be released.

[5 minutes]

When you are sure that the scene has been reframed to your satisfaction, let it go. Bring your attention back to the present moment. Take a deeper breath and be aware of your body once again. Picture yourself surrounded by a bubble of light to protect you. Then, when you are ready, open your eyes.

If appropriate, you can follow this exercise up by tacking up reminders to yourself. Phrase these in positive mode: 'I am free from the past' is preferable to 'I am no longer bound by the past'. If the promise was to a soulmate, then discuss your visualisation to bring things out into the open. You may well find that your soulmate too would like an opportunity to reframe the past. Or it could bring up hidden issues between you that need to be explored.

'The mystic marriage'

One of the strongest soul bonds of all was created in the ancient temples. The mystic marriage was meant to last 'for ever'. An Egyptian papyrus still exists with the steps for making the mystic marriage set out – unfortunately, or fortunately, depending on how you look at it, the last steps are missing. This was a carefully coordinated joining on the physical, emotional, mental and spiritual levels. The couple developed their psychic powers together; telepathy was a fact of mind, as were out of the body experiences. It took years. Both parties had to be ready: one could not advance without the other. Once the souls were joined on all these levels, they were intended to stay together throughout eternity. They had spiritual work to do. Work that would not cease with death.

Such contacts have a powerful hold and may lie at the base of many soulmate feelings. The participants were taught telepathy and soul contact. So, at least one of the partners in a former mystic marriage will usually know exactly what the 'other half' is doing in present-day life even though they are far apart. We saw the present-life effect of a mystic marriage by W.B.Yeats and Maud Gonne – one which may have been a repeat of an earlier union. Some participants have not even met yet in their current life but still they share experiences. Comments vary from 'We met in our dreams long before we met physically' to 'There hasn't been a moment since we met that I did not know exactly what he was thinking and feeling even when I was on the other side of the world', and 'I hated the feeling that he knew every thought I had, and even that he could be controlling them to make me behave in a certain way'. Whilst it may be romantic and wonderful to 'feel as he is feeling, think as she is thinking', this can get in the way of individual development. After a time most people feel invaded by the other person and simply want to put up some boundaries – and, of course, the present life meeting may have exactly that purpose. If the partnership is too symbiotic, separation may be essential. As Plato pointed out, when two souls are totally entwined with each other, death is often the result.

What confuses the issue even further is that it is possible to have made more than one mystic marriage over several lifetimes – or to have made it for that one incarnation only but failed to specify that. Even an arranged marriage in cultures that called for this can act as a mystic marriage in holding people together. A spiritual divorce may well be called for. You may need to see yourself making that vow but with the proviso: 'for this life only', or 'for as long as appropriate.'

A different, more positive and present-life growth-enhancing, kind of mystical marriage is the marriage of our own inner male and female. This can be seen as uniting the various parts of oneself that have been male and female in other lives, or uniting the anima and animus we have carried, or as bringing together the two halves that Plato says were split so long ago. It unites all our masculine and feminine qualities and brings us into inner wholeness. Making this mystical marriage can be a step in our spiritual evolution. It means we no longer have to look 'out there' for our perfect partner. We find all the qualities within ourself.

As a step along the way, we may meet the perfect partner 'out there' – our soulmate – who mirrors to us the unseen and unrecognised part of our soul, but, at some stage, we then move to seeing that part in our inner self. This is the moment when our soulmate must leave, or at least stand aside long enough for the inner union to take place. Then we can go into relationship not as a lopsided person looking for someone to make us whole, but as a whole person who has something to offer in relationship: the unique self of our true being.

The integration of the inner mystic marriage can be encouraged by a simple visualisation.

Exercise: Making the inner marriage

When you are comfortably settled, close your eyes. Take ten slow, deep breaths. As you breathe out, let go of any tension you may be feeling. As you breathe in, draw in a sense of peace and relaxation. Consciously let go of your everyday worries and concerns and allow yourself to be at peace.

Now breathe gently, establishing an even rhythm. Allow your eyelids to grow heavy and lie softly. Then let waves of relaxation flow through your body with each breath. Draw your attention deep inside yourself, allowing the outside world to simply slip away.

When you are ready, picture yourself standing in the entrance to a vast temple. Before you, you can see the huge walls with their high, ornate gates. These are the gates to the inner courtyard. Slowly these gates will open inwards. A temple servant beckons you in.

[2 minutes]

The servant will conduct you to a chamber in the inner courtyard. In this chamber a bath has been prepared. Servants will bathe, dry and perfume you and dress you in new robes to prepare you for your marriage.

[3 minutes]

When you are ready, the servant will then take you to the offering chamber. Here you can make an offering to ensure a successful inner marriage. Whatever is most appropriate for you to offer up will be on the altar before you.

[3 minutes]

Now the servant will take you into the bridal chamber to await your partner in this inner marriage. Food is prepared, drink awaits you. Behind thin, gauzy curtains your marriage bed awaits. When the servant withdraws, your partner will come to you. This will be a total merging, a marriage on all levels. Allow your inner partner to come into your heart, to merge with you.

[10 minutes]

It is now time to leave the bridal chamber. The temple servant will come to conduct you back to the doors leading back into the outside world. Walk with the servant across the courtyard.

[2 minutes]

As you step out of the gates, know that you are whole within yourself. You have integrated your masculine and feminine energies. No longer will you need to look outside yourself for the complementary energy, it is within yourself.

As you stand outside the temple, picture yourself surrounded and protected by a ball of white light. Then take time to slowly bring your attention back to your physical body. Breathe a little more deeply, move your hands and feet. Gradually bring your attention back into the room and get up slowly. Standing with your feet on the floor, picture a grounding cord going from your feet deep down into the earth to hold you in incarnation. Then move around to become fully alert and back in everyday reality.

If you find that the inner partner who appears is someone known to you in your everyday life, check out most carefully whether this really is your true inner partner. Projection, wishful thinking or someone else's intense desire can affect who you see. Do not make the inner marriage unless you are sure. If you make the mystic marriage with someone who is in your life now, be sure to say 'For as long as is appropriate'. It can be a powerful unifying force bringing the two of you together on all levels, and may be just what your relationship needs. Then again, it may not.

Spiritual divorce

What God hath joined together no man ever shall put asunder. God will take care of that.
—*George Bernard Shaw.*

Listening to people, I sometimes get the feeling that God was having a day off when a marriage was supposedly blessed by him. Shaw's ironic comment can be taken two ways, and all too often we do find that what seemed to be a marriage made in heaven was actually conceived in hell. The pregnancy just took a little time to come to fruition and deliver the demons.

So, what do you do when you find yourself in an impossible position? Well, there is something called the karma of grace that says when you have done all you can, you can leave without incurring more karma. Nor do you have to go on paying over and over again for a single mistake:

> *It is by no means necessary to do penance for a lifetime*
> *on account of one karmic debt*
> —*Pauline Stone*[44]

Of course, you do have to be certain that you have done all you can and are not merely running away – that your partner, or ex-soulmate, really is not prepared to work with you in this present lifetime. If this is the case, it is possible to seek a spiritual divorce. It may also be that it was not your soul's intention to be with that person in this lifetime, in which case the divorce may well have to extend back into a past life. This technique is also useful where you feel, or know, you have made a mystic marriage in the past and no longer wish this to bind you. If you know the synastry of your astrological charts, you may find several Neptune and Node contacts with the personal planets. This is a good indication that a spiritual divorce may be called for if all is not going smoothly with your soulmate.

Exercise: The spiritual divorce
(Follow the relaxation instructions in earlier exercises)

When you are in a relaxed state, picture yourself entering a temple or a church. (Allow the picture to come rather than thinking about which it should be.) Notice how you are dressed, are you bride or widow? Either may be appropriate.

You are there to meet with your soulmate (or marriage partner). You have come before a priest (or priestess) to have the breaking of your union blessed. If you are wearing a ring, take it off and return it to the priest.

Looking at each other, rescind the vows that you have made. Take back all those promises. If necessary, let the tears flow as you do so. Where healing and forgiveness are required, let these pass between you.

Say quite clearly: 'I divorce you, I set you free. I become whole again.' The priest (or priestess) will then bless your dis-union, allowing the divine energies to flow over you both bringing more healing and forgiveness.

Then say goodbye to your soulmate, or partner. Wish them well in their future. Accept their blessing and good wishes for your own. If appropriate, forgive yourself for any mistakes you may feel you have made.

Then turn and walk out of the church or temple. Accept the congratulations of those who await you. Be joyous in your separation. This is the moment when you reclaim your soul.

When you are ready to close, surround yourself with a protective bubble of light. Feel yourself whole and healed within that space. Then slowly return your awareness to the room and open your eyes.

Healing the wounds

Is our determination to hang on at all costs really a measure of how much we love?
—*Pauline Stone*[45]

Many people believe that in refusing to let go, they are proving their undying love. I know a woman who has been married fifty-four years. It was a wartime marriage, supposedly the result of love at first sight. She certainly believed she had found her soulmate. She made her vows for eternity. He expected to die at any moment. He made his vows lightly, believing it would all be over soon. He found himself trapped. He still lives his life as though death is the answer, the only thing that can relieve him of this terrible burden called love. For twenty-five of those years, whilst she may have believed herself happy, there was not a day went by when he did not want out. He had many other women. She threatened to commit suicide if he left. Eventually, he did leave her for another woman with whom he still lives. However, neither will divorce the other. It is a classic eternal triangle. For almost thirty years she has sat at home and waited for him to return. She simply cannot not let go. It is as though she is in suspended animation. Her life is on hold. She sees herself as a helpless victim. He experiences her as an all-powerful controlling force who dominates his life even though he has not seen her for thirty years. Only death, she says, can dissolve their union. Only death, he believes, can release him.

So, where do they go from here? What does anyone in this position do? There are certain steps we can all take to heal our relationship wounds, to change the pattern so that it does not carry forward into the future, to rework it so that our relationships become positive, life-enhancing experiences. Whether or not we are already in a soulmate relationship, if we hope to be, or if we have left one behind, we still need to work on our partnership issues. In its simplest form, it comes down to three things: acceptance, forgiveness and letting go,

Believing in karma makes parting a little easier and also helps us to understand why we may be going through some of our less desirable experiences. It can also aid us in ensuring a happier future – after all, what we set in motion now determines the course of the rest of our life (or lives). Understanding our soul's purpose in drawing us into the relationship in the first place also brings us healing insights, as does 'standing in the other person's shoes', seeing it from their point of view. So often, we have a preconception of what we expect from a soulmate: perfect love, shared expectations, certain standards of behaviour, total understanding... The list varies a little from person to person. We seldom look at what we have to offer. Nor do we examine the baggage we bring with us to the relationship: our expectations around love, our ingrained responses, our past experience. Where the preconception and the baggage differ is where we find our pain. So often our response is to try to change the other person, when in reality we can only transform ourselves.

We need to start with our illusions. Is what we are seeking too perfect, too unattainable? Have we set impossible standards? Is what we are seeking really love or some clinging, symbiotic dependence that will suffocate both of us? All of these may need to be re-visioned. Are we seeing ourselves as perfect, not recognising our own all too human flaws and fallibilities? Are we seeing our partner as a god (or goddess)? Do we need to look at their true nature? Do we need to be disillusioned – a painful process but a very necessary one if we are to see what really is. We may be putting onto our partner an heroic, idealised role that simply cannot be fulfilled. We project our aspirations for ourselves onto others; we invest in them what we are not ready to own in ourselves. We may need to take back this projection. To see ourselves, as well as them, as we really are.

We may need to break dependence and passivity, to take back our power and individuality, to recognise that we do indeed make our own future. We may also need to see where we dominate and control, where we seek to have power over the other person, where we manipulate. If we only see one side, we can never heal. We have to offer loving acceptance to ourselves, as well as to our partner.

If we allow our partner simply to be who they are, to accept the worst, as well as recognising the best, then they have a space in which to flower. If we accept what is instead of wishing for more or better, then maybe we will find that we have all we need. If we constantly condemn, what hope is there? In the same way, we need to learn from mistakes instead of condemning them. This is how we grow.

If we let go of karma, step off the eternal round, things change. If we refrain from retaliation, don't strike back, choose not to react, we can transform the pattern. If we let go of our most powerful emotions – grief, anger, compulsion – we create a space for love.

In letting go of those we love most, we allow them to fly, to be, to grow. And, we leave a space for them to come back too. If we hold on tightly, we strangle and suffocate. If we let go, we are being truly loving.

If we have been hurt, if we grieve, if we are angry, our greatest tool is forgiveness. It sets both of us free. If we hold onto those feelings, no one benefits. They are death-dealing instead of life-enhancing. Forgiveness, on the other hand, creates new possibilities. In that space, we may well find all we have ever sought. But if we do not, well then, we can be okay with that too. In a state of need, all we can do is attract neediness. In a state of incompletion, all we can find is an inexact fit. From a position of completeness, we can go into true relationship.

Forgiveness

Guilt and resentment are deeply debilitating. Both occur frequently in soulmate relationships. We tend to know when someone else is holding on to one of these emotions, but we may be less clear when we are. Having said somewhere in the past: 'It's all my/your fault', or 'I'll never forgive you' are clear indications that you may still be holding on, even though you have forgotten, at a conscious level, what it was all about. Whether you were on the receiving end, or gave it out, it is very freeing to go back to these moments and consciously let go. If you do find something for which you would like to make reparation, it may be possible to apologise to the person in person, to drop them a line, send them some flowers, perform a service for someone else which you dedicate to the object of your guilt.

All too often though, you have lost track of the person – or you might not want to approach them at all. If this is the case, it can nevertheless be freeing to write an apology or a letter of forgiveness, using a photograph of the person or a 'mind picture' to link up. Once you have expressed your feelings, you can either tear up the letter or burn it and let the cosmos take it where it needs to go. You can release guilt by lighting a candle and, as it burns away, seeing all your guilt dissolve in the flame. You can follow this up with flower essences (see Appendix II).

A simple visualisation will also help you to give and receive forgiveness. If you are giving forgiveness, you will need to write a letter setting out your love and forgiveness for the other person, although you could also speak from your heart.

Exercise: Giving and receiving forgiveness

Settle yourself in a comfortable, relaxed posture. Close your eyes and breathe gently, concentrating your mind on the area immediately above and between the eyebrows.

When you are ready, picture in your mind the person from whom you wish to receive forgiveness or the person to whom you are giving forgiveness (if this is difficult, use a photograph).

When you have a strong image of this person, either picture yourself reading out your letter and the other person receiving it in a loving, kindly way. Or, picture the other person reading their letter to you and open yourself to them in loving forgiveness.

When the letter reading is finished, ask them to forgive you and allow yourself to feel that forgiveness flowing towards you and into your heart. At the same time, let your forgiveness flow towards them. Allow the forgiveness to spread through your body in a warm glow. Let it settle in your heart.

When the forgiveness is complete, thank the person, wish them well and make any gesture you feel is appropriate, such as hugging or shaking hands.

Then allow them to fade from your mind, sending them on their way with love. Notice how much lighter you feel now that you have given and received forgiveness.

When you are ready, breathe a little more deeply and become aware of your surroundings once more. Then open your eyes slowly.

Non-specific forgiveness

When you are in a relaxed and receptive state, picture in front of you a radiant white light which grows until it completely envelopes you.

This light is all-loving and all-forgiving. Feel it spreading through your body in a warm glow, filling your heart with unconditional, loving acceptance. Rest in its peace until you feel you have been totally forgiven.

Notice how much lighter you feel now that you have received forgiveness.

When you are ready, breathe a little more deeply and become aware of your surroundings once more. Once your attention is back in the room, open your eyes. [Holding a piece of rose quartz on your heart as you do this exercise can greatly strengthen its effect.]

Moving On

We can only find our twin–soul in the integration
of our own inner energies[46]

At a reincarnation conference, I happened to mention I was writing what I laughingly called 'the antidote to soulmates book'. An elderly man came up to me afterwards and anxiously asked: 'Don't you believe in soulmates?' 'Well, yes,' I said, 'But I also believe they can be the exact opposite of what everyone thinks they are looking for.' He told me that twelve years ago he had met his soulmate, now his wife. She had supported him through much depression and many troubles. 'But,' he said, 'There isn't a day goes by when our love does not grow stronger.' Pointing to his heart he said: 'In here I know I have found my soulmate, and she makes my life worth living'.

Such stories do come my way from time to time – just often enough to remind me to adjust the jaundiced view that comes over me when I delve through my postbag. In any one week, there are inevitably three or four letters about soulmates – or the lack of them. One of the most moving plea I hear is: 'Please tell me why my soulmate has moved on and left me behind.'

Lives are irrevocably changed by the loss of a soulmate. In such situations, there are two choices. To carry on as before, or to change. To turn the loss to positive advantage, to make something new happen. Where people try to carry on as before, it is almost as though they are pretending nothing happened. They try to turn back the clock, to re-create the past – often with another soulmate. Or, they enshroud the past, so that it becomes a frozen moment in time devoted to that person's memory. Both responses are death-dealing rather than life-enhancing; nothing moves nor grows.

In two sycophantic books written just after John Lennon's murder,[47] still very much concerned with presenting an idealised picture of soulmates, Yoko Ono was portrayed as being in a deep depression, having 'a full-time job living with John's memory', speaking of John in the present tense as though he had just popped out of the room. She appeared not to have taken in the fact that he was dead. She enshrouded John's memory in song: the broken glasses he was wearing when he died became the front cover for her new album. At the time, she denied that she had a new partner. But in much later, far more realistic accounts,[48] it was alleged that, having sent John away 'on holiday' to Bermuda, Yoko had been all set to divorce him and marry someone else.

However, when John returned with a solo album full of the first new songs he had written for five years (and with plans for the first album to be recorded without Yoko for a long time), she hastily scrapped her intention and insisted on recording *Double Fantasy*, matching song for song with him. According to these authors, Yoko had always used John to further her own recording ambitions. They also revealed that her 'new man' moved in just days after John's death, with Yoko immediately taking up the reins of promoting the album she and John had just recorded. No doubt the truth lies somewhere in between and we will never know for sure. But what is certain is that, well over thirteen years later, sixty-two-year-old Yoko Ono was touring Britain on stage with her singer-son Sean Ono-Lennon: things had turned full circle. She was back on the road again.

Just when I was in the middle of this book, and beginning to feel I needed some positive, life-affirming soulmate experiences to add to what I had already written, I 'happened' to meet an old friend. She was looking radiant and said she had met a man:

Remember you told me it would take time and to wait for the right person because he was there and would come unexpectedly into my life? [She had consulted me some two years previously.] Well, I went out to see Mother Meera in Germany. Suddenly a man came up to me and said he would give me a lift back to the station in the next town. A friend had told him I was going to call a cab. We chatted like old friends as we drove to the town and, as I got out, we exchanged phone numbers. I casually said: 'Give me a ring when you are in town and perhaps we can have a drink.' As he is an American pilot, this was possible but not imminent. Two days later he rang me and said: 'How about that drink?' 'Oh, does that mean you are in London,' I asked. 'No', he said, 'I'm coming over specially to take you out.

The relationship has progressed from there. He's been over to see me several times and I've been to see him in the States. I'm going over for Christmas. We both feel we have things to teach each other. Our beliefs go along the same pathway, and although we are both independent people with a life of our own, we fit together well. I have never felt so much for a man before, never been so loved by a man. I really do feel I have met my soulmate and it will be a positive experience.

This was an enormous turnaround in her life. Her marriage had ended a few years previously, very unhappily, after almost thirty years of devoted service to her husband and his career. At the end, she 'felt like a non-person'. She had picked up the pieces, trained for a new career and was beginning to carve out a place for herself where she could be of service to others and fulfil herself at the same time. She had met great personal tragedy since her marriage broke up. She had lost, in different ways, two soulmates. A beloved grandchild had died and her much loved son had had to be hospitalised with a psychiatric condition that seemed intractable.

She had had to deal with great guilt around this son, with whom she had a soulmate relationship of deep understanding. He had had a difficult relationship with his father, who took no further interest in him. To compensate, she gave him a great deal of her time and energy. She had badgered the doctors in an attempt to find the best treatment for him, and had so investigated the condition as to become something of an expert. Prior to meeting her future partner, she had done considerable work on letting her son go, to be the person he needed to be. Indeed, she had gone to Mother Meera with the specific intention of leaving him in the hands of the Great Mother. This, she felt, had been beneficial to their relationship; they were 'not so symbiotic now'. It created space for another soulmate to enter her life, one with whom she could have a full relationship, one with whom she could move into the future with confidence.

So, if we change our attitude to love and loving, we can change what we attract in the way of a soulmate. Our relationships may still be difficult, but they will be different. It may well be that we now have something to offer our soulmate, a chance for them to grow. One of my clients, who had worked hard on accepting herself and on changing her way of loving, felt that it was time to find a soulmate. As she said, she had a good life, one that was rich and satisfying, but she felt she would like a partner. Thinking it over carefully, she advertised. Her advert was different. Instead of listing what she was looking for, she set out what she felt she had to offer. Her argument was that this would then attract someone who was looking for the qualities she had to give. Sure enough, she met a man with whom she had much in common. They got on extremely well.

There was only one problem. He had never had a long-term committed relationship. He always had several women on the go 'to be on the safe side'. Having the belief within himself that he was not lovable, he expected to be hurt in relationships. So, he would do all he could to push away his partners. He could then say: 'See, I knew it.' My client was wise to this game, she had played it for years. So, when he tried to push her away, she simply said: 'I'll always be here. It doesn't matter what you do, I love you and I'll be here for you.' Gradually, he began to trust her. Finally, he asked her to go to Australia – his home – with him on a trial visit. He wanted to see how things would work out. She agreed to go for six months, not to see how things worked out with him, but to see if she could make a life for herself there which would enable her to be in relationship with him. She is still there:

I'm in no hurry to try to formalise a lifestyle – will I ever be again, I wonder! I'm simply enjoying the journey very much: it is bringing me riches and pleasures I had only glimpsed before. All I can say is that it feels very right to be here, it feels very right to be here with Peter and the future will take its own course as we develop it by living fully in the present.

When I contacted her for permission to use her story she said:

We are both very happy for you to do so. On this journey I'm learning a great deal about myself. Having opened my heart so fully, the vulnerable child seems often to be present... Also his vulnerable child is often evoked, as though in our openness to one another we inhabit some of our deepest hurts. The important thing is that we are both then able to understand what is happening, thus taking back the projections. It's bloody hard work at times but also very life-enhancing. It really feels like we've been drawn together for the lessons we each need to learn.

The other women in his life have disappeared completely. Peter is very clear about his commitment and revels in his new status. He says now he feels fulfilled, like he's come home and he has absolutely no desire for anything or anyone else.

Learning to live with someone again after years of fierce independence is interesting! (a euphemism for rewarding, challenging, joyous, scary and hopeful). This is true for both of us as we learn to communicate and adjust; to be both interdependent and independent; to understand and be understood. Wish us well as we continue our separate and joint journeys.

So, it seems that the key to resolving the soulmate enigma is to move beyond our expectations and demands, to let go of our dreams, and simply to live each day as it comes. Accepting whatever a relationship offers in whatever way it presents itself whilst at the same time maintaining our own inner 'rightness'. This is the gift our soulmate offers. Whether we accept it or not is up to us.

Our difficulties from the past are often, seemingly, inextricably linked to people with whom we have become 'enmeshed' and with whom we have created bonds which are not always good for us. This is particularly true in love relationships but can apply to any interaction. I use a method of 'cutting the ties' which is closely linked to, but not based on, the work of Phyllis Krystal. It involves letting go of all the 'oughts, shoulds and if-only's' which make our contact with people conditional and which hold us, and them, back from developing as people in our own right.

Cutting can be carried out with anyone regardless of whether they are still alive or active in your life, which makes it perfect for releasing people from other lives, as well as present life, parents, ex-husbands or lovers. It is useful to do this exercise with a soulmate from time to time, even if you are in a happy relationship as it keeps it clear and working well. The Australian Bush Essences Stuart Desert Pea and Sunshine Wattle aid in letting go the past, and the Bach Flower Essences Walnut and Honeysuckle are helpful in cutting the ties and can be taken prior to the cutting and for several days following. The Australian essence Boab is indispensable for breaking family patterns.

The work involves cutting the emotional ties that have built up and sets both parties free to be themselves and to take their own place in life. **It does not cut off the love**, but it does remove all the conditions, the 'oughts, shoulds, buts and if-only's', which can attach themselves to what masquerades as 'love'. For rather too many people 'loving' their children or partner involves a subtle radiation of acceptance or non-acceptance based on whether the other person is conforming to what is required or considered to be 'good'. Love, unfortunately, is all too often a method of control. Paradoxically, in letting go, the bond of love often becomes stronger and the relationship improves as the other person is perceived as a person in their own right. The imaging is also useful for working with people, such as parents or grandparents, whom you have loved very much but who have now passed on, as they can still be having a deep influence in your life and you may still be living out their hopes for you.

As the visualisation frees you from the past, and particularly from people that have been holding you back without your realising it, it can be helpful to do a 'blank' cutting, creating the circle and then asking that whoever you most need to cut away from will appear in the circle.

This work is powerful and should only be undertaken if you really feel it is right. I have already documented in *The Karmic Journey*[49] the case of a woman who had an adult, drug-addict son with whom she was inextricably enmeshed and with whom she unconsciously colluded in order to keep him dependent on her. She believed he was her true soulmate. She attended a Phyllis Krystal workshop and, although she intellectually understood that the exercise was designed not to cut off love, she was ambivalent because deep down inside herself she believed that in cutting the ties she would cut off the support she felt he needed from her (a good example of not being properly in touch with her true feelings, and also of the mistake of confusing 'support' with 'love' which so many mothers make). This was a case of her head saying one thing, and her heart another. Nevertheless, as she was on the workshop, she started to do the cutting. She 'fell asleep' in the middle but told no one. She had seen the tie as a 'tree-trunk' linking her to her son, which she had begun to cut away from her navel with a scalpel. A few days later, her navel was raw and bleeding and she came to me to complete the cutting. She slept for twelve hours immediately following its completion, during which time her navel healed.

It has been suggested that this exercise may interfere with another person's autonomy and rights. However, the meadow, in the visualisation, represents your own inner space. In doing this exercise, you are inviting another person to manifest in that inner space. They are there by your invitation, not by right (although they may well already occupy part of that space without your invitation, which interferes with your own autonomy). By using the circles you delineate the space which each of you can occupy while doing the work. You should not let the circles overlap, or allow the other person to move into your circle. When the work is complete, you set them free and send them back to their own place. In other words, they move out of your inner space and into their own. Thus, you are each set free to inhabit your own space.

The meditation is set in a meadow, but some people find it easier to picture the sea-shore, the side of a lake, or some other peaceful place. It is important to use your own images, rather than ones I suggest to you, so adapt the wording if necessary. During the imaging work, the ties can manifest in many ways, as nets, hooks, umbilical cords, etc. – and in many places. It is quite common to find a sexual tie linking you to a father or brother or even to your mother. These images are the subconscious mind's way of symbolically representing an emotional and psychic truth and should be accepted as such. Part of the work involves removing the ties, the place where they have been on each person being healed and sealed with light, and the other part involves destroying these ties. I find the most useful way of doing this is to have a large fire, as again the symbolism is important. As the fire burns, it transmutes the tie into energy. It is also possible to use water to dissolve or wash away the ties. The one method I do not recommend is to bury them, as symbolically this does not free you from them, and they may well sprout and grow again. Having said that, I have learned from years of experience that it is impossible to be dogmatic as, just occasionally, a tie may be transformed through death and rebirth, of which the ritual of burying can be a part.

Exercise: Tie-cutting visualisation

Take time to relax and settle, breathing gently. Then picture yourself walking in a meadow on a nice, warm, sunny day. Really let yourself feel the grass beneath your feet, the cool earth below. There is a gentle breeze playing around your face, keeping you cool and comfortable.

Spend a little time exploring your meadow and then choose the spot where you want to do this work.

Draw a circle around yourself as you stand in the meadow. The circle should be at arms length and go right around you. You can use paint, chalk, light or whatever comes to mind. This circle delineates your space. (If you use a hoop of light, it can be pulled up around you if needed.)

In front of you, close to but not touching your circle, draw another circle the same size. Picture the person with whom you wish to cut the ties in the circle. (If you have difficulty in seeing the person clearly, you can picture a photograph being placed in the circle.) Do not let the circles overlap; peg them down if necessary.

Explain to the person why you are doing this exercise. Tell them that you are not cutting off any unconditional love there may be, but that you wish to be free from the old emotional conditioning and bonds that built up in the past, and any expectations in the present.

Look to see how the ties symbolically manifest themselves. Then spend time removing them, first from yourself, healing and sealing the places where they were with light; then removing them from the other person. Make sure you get all the ties, especially the ones around the back which you may overlook. Pile the ties up outside the circle.

When you are sure you have cleared all the ties, and sealed all the places where they have been, let unconditional love, forgiveness and acceptance (where possible) flow between you and the other person. Then let that other person go back to where they belong.

Gather up all the ties and find an appropriate way of destroying them. You may wish to have a large bonfire onto which you throw them, or a swiftly flowing river into which you cast them. Make sure you have destroyed all the ties.

If you are using a fire, move nearer to the flames and feel the transmuted energy warming, purifying, healing and energising you, filling all the empty spaces left by removing the ties. This is your own creative life force coming back to you in its released and purified form. Absorb as much of this energy as you need. If you feel able to, move into the fire and become like the phoenix, reborn from the flames.

If you are using water, you might like to enter the water, or to use the heat of the sun to purify, heal and energise yourself. Then wrap a bubble of light around you to protect yourself.

Repeat the cutting with another person if you wish. When you have completed all the cutting you wish to do, bring your attention back into the room and allow yourself plenty of time to readjust, breathing more deeply and bringing yourself into full awareness with feet firmly on the ground.

Appendix Two
Flower Essences for Relationships

Flower essences are a very gentle way of healing and dissolving old pain and bringing about a positive outcome. The essences are supplied either in a stock bottle from which a few drops are added to a bottle of brandy and water mix, or in dosage bottles ready for use. Purpose-made combination essences (which do not need to be diluted) are available. The usual dose is seven drops twice daily. As well as being taken personally, essences can be used to help other people by dropping them onto a crystal placed on a photograph.

Karma Clear: Findhorn Flower Essences
For releasing pain from the past and understanding the deep-rooted cause of problems. Releases the attachments which bring about pain, unhappiness and dis-ease. It contains:

- Birch: to bring insight into the past
- Snowdrop: to offer new hope and detachment
- Rowan: to release resentment, heal old wounds, support forgiveness
- Holy-Thorn: to open to true intimacy and bring unconditional love

Spiritual Marriage: Findhorn Flower Essences
This is particularly useful when making the inner marriage as it integrates dualities such as head-heart, mind-love, male-female. It brings about harmony and union and the joy of right relationship. It contains:

- ♥ Apple: to free the creative willpower
- ♥ Holy-Thorn: to open the heart to love and intimacy and expression of the true self
- ♥ Seapink: to bring harmony of energy flow

Relationship Essence: Australian Bush Essences

This essence has been made to enhance the quality of all relationships, especially intimate ones. Includes seven essences as seven represents learning lessons, forgiveness and expression of love:

- ♥ Bluebell: to release blocked emotions and open the heart, to encourage sharing
- ♥ Bush Gardenia: to revitalise relationships, increase communication and enhance romance and passion
- ♥ Dagger Hakea: to release resentment and bring about forgiveness and honest expression of feelings
- ♥ Mint Bush: to resolve chaos and confusion, especially when deciding to leave or to stay
- ♥ Red Suva Frangipani: to heal emotional pain and turmoil. to work on the heart centre when a relationship ends
- ♥ Boab: to break early family conditioning and patterns, and to avoid projection onto a partner
- ♥ Flannel Flower: to express feelings, create healthy boundaries and enjoy physical contact

Sexuality Essence: Australian Bush Essences

Specially made to heal sexual and relationship trauma and to bring about openness to sensuality and touch. It also helps with physical and emotional intimacy. It contains:

- ♥ Flannel Flower: to bring about intimacy and enjoyment of touch
- ♥ Bush Gardenia: to renew passion and an interest in the relationship
- ♥ Billy Goat Plum: to release shame and to enhance body image.
- ♥ Wisteria: to heal abuse and overcome frigidity, leading to gentleness and openness in relationships
- ♥ Fringed violet: to heal trauma and shock

Other essences which may help with relationship difficulties are:

- ♥ Bottlebrush and Boronia(Bush): to help let go and heal a broken heart
- ♥ Chicory (Bach): to release over-possessiveness and self-pity
- ♥ Little Flannel Flower (Bush): to encourage playfulness and fun
- ♥ Mountain Devil (Bush): to clear grudges, resentment and hatred
- ♥ Pine (Bach): to clear guilt
- ♥ Pink Mulla Mulla (Bush): helps loners who feel isolated
- ♥ Rowan (Findhorn): to bring about forgiveness
- ♥ Sunshine Wattle (Bush): to release people who are stuck in the past
- ♥ Stuart Desert Pea (Bush): to heal deep hurt and sadness and help in letting go and finding forgiveness
- ♥ Stuart Desert Rose (Bush): to release guilt
- ♥ Walnut (Bach): to help change and tie cutting
- ♥ Wedding Bush (Bush): to aid commitment
- ♥ Willow (Bach): to clear resentment

Further reading:

White, Ian: *Bush Flower Essences* – Findhorn Press
Leigh, Marion: *Findhorn Flowere Essences* — Findhorn Press

Essence Supplier:

Findhorn Flower Essences
The Wellspring
31 The Park
Findhorn Bay
Forres IV36 OTZ
Tel. 01309 690129

The Working Tree
Milland
Liphook
Hants GU30 7JS
Tel. 01428 741572

References & Credits

1. Pauline Stone *Relationships, Astrology and Karma* (HarperCollins 1991), p.189. Reprinted by permission of HarperCollins Publishers Ltd.
2. Passed to me by a friend of John Lennon.
3. Richard Bach, *The Bridge Across Forever* (London: Pan, 1985), back cover.
4. Brian Weiss, *Only Love is Real* (London: Piatkus, 1996), p.148.
5. Rabindranath Tagore, *Later Poems*, trans. Aurobino Bose (Minerva Press, 1976), p.62.
6. Brian Weiss, *op. cit.*
7. Plato, *Symposium* (London: Penguin 1951), p.61. Reproduced by permission of Penguin Books Ltd.
8. Ibid, p.62.
9. Tom Bridges, article in *The Mountain Astrologer*, Oct 1995, p.22.
10. Pauline Stone, *op. cit.*
11. Thomas Moore, *Soulmates*, (Shaftesbury: Element Books, 1994), p.xviii.
12. Richard Bach, *op. cit.*, p.265.
13. Brian Weiss, *op. cit.*, p.1.
14. Francis Steegmuller, *Your Isadora*, (New York: Random House, 1974), p.279.
15. From *My Life* by Isadora Duncan. Copyright 1927 by Horace Liveright, Inc., renewed © 1955 by Liveright Publishing Corporation. Reprinted by permission of Liveright Publishing Corporation.
16. In personal correspondence but later used in *In the Light of Experience*.
17. Nik Douglas & Penny Slinger, *Sexual Secrets*, (Destiny Books, 1979)
18. Elizabeth Haich, *Initiation*, (London: Mandala Books, 1985).
19. Blaise Pascal, *Penseés* (1670).
20. Stephen Arroyo, *Astrology, Karma and Transformation*, (Vancouver: CRCS, 1978), p.109.
21. Richard Bach, *Illusions*, (London: Pan, 1979), p.121.
22. Mavis Klein – source unknown, believed to be in an article.
23. Frederick Seaman, *The Last Days of John Lennon*, (New York: Birch Lane Press, 1991). Albert Goldman, *The Lives of John Lennon*, (Bantam Books, 1989).
24. Judy Hall, *The Astrology of a Prophet?*, (Mendip Press, 1993) – available from the author.
25. Plato, *op. cit.*, p.62.
26. Ibid, p.62.
27. Ibid, p.62-3.
28. Kahlil Gibran, *The Prophet* (Arcarna, 1992).
29. David Lawson, *The Eye of Horus – An Oracle of Ancient Egypt*, (Piatkus Books).
30. Julie Felix, *You Slept With Her* (© J Felix 1986).
31. Judy Hall.
32. David Icke, *In the Light of Experience*, (London: Thorson, 1993).
33. Mary K Greer, *Women of the Golden Dawn*, (Rochester: Park Street Press, 1995).
    A. Norman Jeffares, *W.B. Yeats Man and Poet*, (London: Kyle Cathie, 1996).
    W.B. Yeats, *Memoirs*, (London: MacMillan, 1972).
    A. Norman Jeffares, *W.B. Yeats A Vision*, (London: Arena, 1990).
    W.B. Yeats, *Autobiographies*, (London: MacMillan, 1980).
    Richard Ellman, *Yeats – the Man and his Masks*, (London: Penguin, 1979).
34. Richard Ellman, op. cit.
35. Personal information from Christine Hartley in 1978.
36. Judy Hall.
37. Judy Hall.

38. Judy Hall.
39. Christopher Marlowe, *Dr Faustus*.
40. Pauline Stone, *op. cit.*
41 W.B. Yeats, *Memoirs*, (London: MacMillan, 1972).
42. Talat Sait et al, *Cedaleddin Rumi and the Whirling Dervishes*, (Turkey: Dost Yayinlan, n.d.).
43. Irina Tweedie, *Daughter of Fire.*
44. Pauline Stone, *op. cit.*
45. Ibid.
46. Judy Hall.
47. Peter Brown and Steven Gains, *The Love You Make*, (Pan Books, 1983), p.392.
    Ray Coleman, *John Lennon*, (Futura, 1985), p.458.
48. Frederick Seaman and Albert Goldman, (London: Penguin, 1990).
49. Judy Hall, *The Karmic Journey*, (London: Penguin, 1990).

Introducing Findhorn Press

Findhorn Press is the publishing business of the Findhorn Community which has grown around the Findhorn Foundation, co-founded in 1962 by Peter and Eileen Caddy and Dorothy Maclean. The first books originated from the early interest in Eileen's guidance over 25 years ago, and Findhorn Press now publishes not only Eileen's books of guidance and inspirational material, but many others. It has also forged links with a number of like-minded authors and organisations.

For further information about the Findhorn Community and how to participate in its programmes, please write to:

The Accommodation Secretary
Findhorn Foundation
Cluny Hill College
Forres IV36 0RD
Scotland
Tel +44 (0)1309 673655 • Fax +44 (0)1309 673113
email reception@findhorn.org
url: http://www.gaia.org/findhorn/index.html/

For a complete catalogue or more information about Findhorn Press products, please contact:

Findhorn Press
The Park, Findhorn, Forres IV36 0TZ, Scotland
Tel +44 (0)1309 690582 • Fax +44 (0)1309 690036
email thierry@findhorn.org
url: http://www.gaia.org/findhornpress/